WHAT PEOPL… ABOUT MORT MEISNER

"I've known Mort Meisner for over 40 years. I knew him first professionally, when we worked together at the ABC television station in Detroit, Michigan. I've known him continually since then as a friend and sometimes colleague at other stations. To me, Mort has always been a bigger-than-life character. I hope this book will give the reader a small sense of why. I know of no one who worked with more passion and enthusiasm as a television newsman. He had a 'Rolodex' memory for contacts and knew how to reach them. That's of indispensable value in a newsroom.

But, it was outside the newsroom that Mort's true life stories and incredible experiences engendered sorrow, fascination, and enjoyment. You'll find those stories here. Finally, other than my wife, there is no one to whom I would rather turn if in trouble, pain, or need. As the author C.S. Lewis once wrote, 'Friendship is the greatest of worldly goods.' This is a book about that."

Steve Antoniotti
Former General Manager, WJBK FOX Detroit

"I have had a highly enjoyable working relationship with Mort for years—first coaching his talent at Fox2 Detroit and then coaching some of his many TV clients. We admire and appreciate his direct, no-nonsense approach; he tells it EXACTLY like it is. Mort is tenacious, determined, super-sharp, caring, generous, and a whirling dervish—working the phones and managing his many projects with great efficiency. His audaciously colorful and crazy-making life could not be contained in just one book!"

Joni Brander
Broadcast Talent Coach, thetvcoach.com, Chicago

"A no-holds-barred look at big city TV news in its heyday. Mort Meisner tells of the highs and lows of running a news operation in major markets like Chicago, Detroit, and St. Louis. Meisner minces no words as he also grapples with a drug habit that almost takes him down. *Enough to be Dangerous* is a great read."

John "Bulldog" Drummond
Former Mob & Crime Reporter
CBS O&O WBBM, Chicago

"I could not put it down. So compelling, honest, and helpful. A book that had to be written—because anyone who witnessed what you will read here certainly needed to write a book about it. A compelling story of struggles, determination, compassion—and love. And to be clear—as he does in life—Mort tells it like it is! No excuses! A heartfelt look at one's life from within that may just leave you asking...what have I accomplished... what have I done to learn from experiences and work to make this a better place?"

Murray Feldman
Former Business and Finance Anchor/Reporter,
FOX, WJBK Detroit
WWJ News Radio 950

"I have watched first-hand the metamorphosis of Mort Meisner over the last 21 years. Mort is a smart man and has learned to play to his strengths as he has addressed his shortcomings. Mort's personal story along with his career stories are must reading and something all of us can learn from."

Dr. Norman Goldner, Ph.D

"I was fortunate to work with Mort Meisner during some of the most momentous and evolutionary years in Detroit television news. You will be given an insight into many of these notable events and personalities in the pages of this memoir."

Jerry Hodak
Meteorologist/Health and Science Reporter
ABC, WXYZ Detroit

"How did he do it? How did he always bring enthusiasm and passion to the work whether it was investigating a story or developing a talent? This book answers the question: with focus, self-reliance, and sheer will to succeed against all odds. It never was and never is boring to work with Mort Meisner."

Kathryn Kiefer
TV News Talent Coach
Former TV NEWS ANCHOR/REPORTER
WXYZ, Detroit; WBBM, Chicago; KGO, San Francisco;
KMGH, Denver; WBZ, Boston; KTVI, St. Louis

"Mort Meisner is a one-of-a-kind, caring, and thoughtful guy who gets straight to the point. Hearing and reading about his experiences has been wildly entertaining, and sometimes mind blowing. He's not only funny but his stories are memorable and worth sharing as life lessons."

Jason Knowles
Consumer Investigative Reporter
ABC, WLS Chicago

"*Enough to be Dangerous* takes us on quite a ride! Mort gives us a peek behind the curtains of the music business, the news business, and into the heart of a man who could have been defeated by a tragic upbringing but instead stuck to his passion and created quite a life! Mort acknowledges mentors who had been instrumental to him over the years. And then Mort gives back, mentoring so many himself and being a true force of positive change for black journalists. A great read!"

Diana Lewis
Anchor/Reporter
ABC, WXYZ Detroit

"I thought I knew Mort Meisner, former boss, and longtime friend. Then I read his book. Wow, what an eye-opener! Mort bares all in a gripping tale of child abuse, sex, drugs, booze and rock 'n' roll. Plus, amazing inside stories about the underbelly of TV news."

Scott Lewis
Award Winning Former Investigative Reporter
FOX O&O, WJBK Detroit
Private Investigator and Owner, Scott Lewis Investigations

"Mort Meisner's deep-dive behind the scenes of television news during its heyday will shock and surprise. This brutally honest portrayal of major market news anchors and reporters, and the culture he describes, replete with troubling examples of racism, sexism, and widespread drug use, makes Meisner more than 'enough to be dangerous' to the legacy of television news."

Jay Levine
Reporter, CBS Owned & Operated WBBM, Chicago

"I have known Mort Meisner for 35 years. He is one of the most positive individuals who possesses a broader picture of the world and of the common man. Mort's story will grab your heart, touch your soul, and you will love every page."

Isaiah "Ike" Mckinnon, Ph.D
Former Detroit Police Chief/Deputy Mayor

"I've known Mort Meisner for decades. As a talent agent he is fiercely loyal, always stood FOR me, always stood WITH me. A relentless advocate. As a friend, he is incredibly loyal, the kind of person you call when you achieve something great and, the kind of friend you call when you are really hurting. He's rock steady. Not just me, but my wife and family revere him because they know this about his guidance and goodness: 'I'm with Mort.'"

Craig Nigrelli
Anchor/Reporter
KAKE, Wichita

"Mort Meisner mentored decades of successful American television journalists. He empowered individuals with the confidence to effectively communicate while being fair and factual. Most pronounced was Mort's desire to beat the competition and win the newscast ratings period with a mantra, I can still hear clearly today, 'Need it, want it, get it, Period.' Guess who's still winning in 2020, 'Exclamation Point.'"

John Pertzborn
Anchor/Reporter
FOX, KTVI St. Louis

"Managing a television newsroom is not for the timid. I can attest to that. I'm a former news director. The job is exhilarating but daunting to the extreme. Before becoming a talent agent for some of the biggest names in television news, Mort Meisner ran the biggest newsrooms in the country deftly and with style. He made it look easy. Mort conquered much tougher demons. He rose strong above an abusive childhood and hardcore drug use. Most mere mortals would have crumbled. How could someone with such a traumatic past become such a positive force, such an optimist, such a major success? Mort answers that and many other questions in his memoir *Enough to be Dangerous.* Mort is a great storyteller and a colorful personality. He'll entertain you with tales from inside the television newsroom and you'll learn how his past fueled his future. Time is precious. You won't waste a minute. Read Mort's story – it's captivating."

Joe Rovitto
Clemensen Rovitto, LLC
TV Consultants

ENOUGH TO BE DANGEROUS

ONE AGENT'S LIFE IN TV NEWS AND ROCK & ROLL

Mort Meisner
with Stephanie Ruopp

For information about this title or to order other books and/or for bulk orders, contact the publisher:

Two Sisters Writing and Publishing
DBA Atkins & Greenspan Publishing
18530 Mack Avenue, Suite 166
Grosse Pointe Farms, MI 48236
www.twosisterswriting.com

ISBN 978-1-945875-77-9 Hardcover
ISBN 978-1-945875-78-6 Paperback
ISBN 978-1-945875-79-3 eBook

Printed in the United States of America
Cover and Interior design: Leslie Mangas
Front cover photo: Glenn Triest

DEDICATION

To my children: Jason, Nicole, and Mark Meisner; and to my grandchildren: Tony Meisner, Bruce Meisner-Brooks, and all my future grandchildren, this story is dedicated to you. You are my heart, my soul, my love, and my world.

This story is also dedicated to everyone out there struggling in life, whether with a substance or an emotional issue.

To journalists everywhere trying to make a difference, this is dedicated to you. There are thousands of you. Journalism is under attack. Whether you are a TV news, radio, print, or online journalist, continue to do everything possible to get the story right and to always be fair. Haters who call your reporting fake news should be dismissed as sour grapes at best and running scared at worst. Just keep bringing your best every day.

Finally, this story is dedicated to Black and brown people in the United States who still, even in 2020, continue to be treated as second-class citizens—if not something worse.

A change still has to come. As Langston Hughes wrote: "Let America be America again. Let America be the dream the dreamers dreamed."

ACKNOWLEDGMENTS

I am immensely grateful for the many people who helped bring this book into being, either directly or by being a guiding light in my life.

Mark Meisner and Alex Steinberg
Title

Nicole Meisner
Social Media

Leslie Mangas
Book Cover Design & Graphic Design

Stephanie Ruopp
Writing

Jim Epperson
Best Friend and Unconditional Love

Nolan Mendenhall
Inspirational and constantly shows me the way

Dr. Keith Khalil
Inspiration

Larry Foote
Friend, Teammate, Confidant since October 13th, 1963
Always there with me through thick and thin

Barbara Goldsmith
Advanced Composition—Best K-12 Teacher

Harry Weberman
High School Counselor. He taught me to believe in myself

Dr. Norman Goldner
Most influential man in my life

1ST FOREWORD

Drenched in sweat, hoarse from singing and screaming, legs weak from dancing and standing for four hours, Mort hugged me, kissed me on the lips and shouted, "Now you've seen Bruce like you're supposed to!"

He had secured fourth-row seats at a Springsteen show in Detroit, a city that embraced The Boss early and since has been rewarded with decades of legendary performances.

"How you feeling?" he asked.

"Dead," I said, then added, "and fully alive." Mort looked at me knowingly, like there was more to say, but the time wasn't right.

Two days later back in St. Louis, the office phone rang. "How you doing, brother?" It was Mort.

"It's funny, Morty," I started. "Well, strange may be a better word," I stammered. "That show was incredible—never seen anything like it. But the last day or so," I paused, looking for the right words. "I feel…" I tried, but just couldn't seem to find the right word.

"Inferior?" Mort said in a snappy, confident clip. "Don't worry, man. Bruce makes everyone feel like that."

I smiled, exhaled slowly for the first time in a while and immediately felt better.

That's Mort—a voice that cuts through the clutter and confusion to get to what matters. I've seen him do it for over 30 years, for me and for countless others who need to make sense of the bewildering hand that life can deal. He's always looking for people who need encouragement, advice, or love from an understanding soul. But it's his ability to lock onto what's eluding us that sets Mort apart. Clarity is his gift. Maybe it's his highly successful years in the TV news business that allow him to ingest enormous amounts of information and frenzied emotion, and almost instantly share a conclusion that brings life and light to dimming eyes.

As you read *Enough To Be Dangerous*, you'll meet a guy who's lived a life of sex, drugs and rock 'n' roll. You'll also learn that Mort personally knows just about every band or act you've ever wanted to see or know more about. That's exciting stuff, to be sure. But that had—and has—nothing to do with how I feel about Mort. It's all about his passion, energy, talent and intelligence—and more than anything, his heart.

I've seen him run down fly balls in left field that were uncatchable; saw him transform our ragtag softball team to a division winner; watched him come to bat with a man on first, yet end the play with Mort on third base and the other guy on second. On a more treacherous field, Mort introduced me to recovery from alcohol and drug addiction; I owe him my life. And he counseled me once, after a rare argument with my Dad, to NEVER let anything come between father and son—advice I followed and especially cherished when Dad slipped away two years ago.

It may not seem to rise to the level of life and death, but Mort also gave me a lasting love for all things Springsteen. On at least three occasions, Bruce has released an album that examined exactly where I was—usually in need of Hope and Dreams. Bruce delivered because Mort delivered—always, every time.

I'll always remember the first time we met face-to-face. We had talked business on the phone several times, but that was all. My wife Debbie knew how impressed I was with Mort, so she invited Leslie and him to my surprise 30th birthday party. I was laughing and talking with friends when Debbie answered the door. Without ever seeing him before, I knew it was Mort when he topped the stairs. It was an instant, intense feeling—a "that's him" moment. It's reminiscent of another fabled introduction.

Springsteen tells about the night he met Clarence Clemons, his sax player, blood brother, and recipient of countless kisses on stage. Bruce was playing a small club as a storm raged outside. Lightning, thunder, wind, and rain almost drowned out the music. When Clarence stepped into the club, wind ripped the door off its hinges and blew it away into the night. And there he stood, filling the empty door frame, sax in hand.

"Mind if I sit in?" he asked Bruce.

"Big Man," Bruce said to him, "you can do anything you want." And then the yet uncrowned Future of Rock thought, *There's my guy.*

I know exactly how he felt.

And you can, too. Put on some Springsteen—maybe *No Retreat, No Surrender*—crank it up and dive into the unique life of Mort Meisner. You'll learn about a man who has done it all. And you'll see a young man I've grown older with, who once was a respected peer, then a friend, then a best friend, then my brother.

"There's my guy."

And he always will be, all the way home.

Jim Epperson
Retired Corporate Officer at AT&T
(President of Mort Meisner Fan Club)

2ND FOREWORD

First of all, it's hard to believe that Mort Meisner is still alive! I've known him for more than 35 years, but I had no idea of the hell he grew up in... or the hell he went through as a young man to survive.

Few of us could have made it through a childhood filled with the physical and psychological abuse Mort and his brother, Tony, had to endure. The post-traumatic stress left its mark, and yet made him stronger, too.

He got his college degree from the University of Detroit Mercy, but his greatest lessons came from the people he encountered in his crazy, mad, wild journey through the industries of music and news.

This book is not a pretty picture of what we might expect to see from the front office of local news operations. It's filled with debauchery and drugs, racism and ridicule, hyperbole and hypocrisy.

But Mort's story is also filled with hope, faith, perseverance, and love.

When you think of some of our era's greatest musicians—Bruce Springsteen, David Bowie, the Ohio Players, KISS—Mort is in the mix. You might even hear his voice on some of your favorite albums.

And when you think of our era's greatest broadcasters—Bill Bonds, Walter Jacobson, and Dave Diles—Mort is also part of the story, tracking down the facts, managing egos, and breaking news.

Some of you may not know his name, but you've seen his work —on concert stages across the region and on television stations in St.Louis, Chicago, and Detroit.

Over the years, I've both loved him and hated him, admired him and despised him.

After all, he was my boss. His decisions had a huge impact on my life and career.

The Mort Meisner who was part of the team that offered me my first major job in television news was also the same man who tried to fire me a few years later.

What you're about to read is raw, real, and shocking. It's a soul-baring, truth-revealing biography of a man who beat the odds, a man who found a way to make peace with his past, overcome his demons, and find joy in his journey.

To paraphrase the words of Bette Davis, "Fasten your seat belts, it's going to be a bumpy ride!" Enjoy!

Huel Perkins
Anchor, Fox 2 News Detroit
Host, Let It Rip!

CONTENTS

PROLOGUE

LESSONS ON RACISM...

NOT READING, WRITING, OR ARITHMETIC ON THE FIRST DAY OF SCHOOL

Terror was pounding my heart and ringing in my ears as I walked toward the crowd of white parents and students who stood waiting—angry, hateful, and ready for a fight—in front of my school.

I gripped my mother's hand as we got closer. All I wanted was to enjoy the first day of second grade, and meet all the new kids who would soon arrive on buses from a nearby neighborhood.

But the angry crowd made it clear that wouldn't go well.

My seven-year-old mind could not comprehend their fury over plans to bus Black students whose school had burned down. To me, it was great that they could come here and attend Edgar Guest Elementary School, named for a poet who celebrated optimism about everyday life.

My naïveté was more like Mr. Guest's philosophy, because I was excited for new kids to join our school and become my friends. In fact, my imagination had spun idyllic visions of smiling children descending the steps of big yellow busses.

Somehow, though, I feared something bad was about to happen.

So far, only one Black student attended Guest, where I'd been going since kindergarten. My classmates were kids from our neighborhood, where we were surrounded by a few other poor Jewish families and, for lack of a more accurate description, what my father called "Southern white trash." Let's just say it was definitely *not* an integrated neighborhood.

And white folks thought that was just fine during the racially tense 1950s. Now it was 1960, and the feeling remained.

Even after fire destroyed McCarroll Elementary, and the students—most of whom were Black—needed a new place to learn.

As a result, the school district hatched a plan to bus McCarroll's students to Guest. Actually, it was the only option. And not a good one, according to our white neighbors.

But at the bright and hopeful age of seven, I thought it would be pretty neat to have a bunch of new kids at school—a whole new crop of potential friends. What could possibly go wrong?

That, plus the fact that my parents were completely on board with the idea, further cemented my faith in the viability of this plan. My dad was especially in favor of it. Not that he was a peaceful and loving person who practiced tolerance and kindness. In fact, he could be a violent and hateful man who was rarely on board with anything.

This was probably the biggest anomaly when it came to my father. Despite the vitriol and wrath that he delivered to my mother, brother, and me with startling regularity, he had no tolerance for bigotry. So he actually praised the notion of his son attending an integrated school. As off-the-hook as my dad was, he supported racial equality and the expansion of civil rights.

"Those damned white trash scissor bills have no right to have a problem with this," he snarled in reference to our many "hillbilly" neighbors. "Those colored kids deserve an education just like you do. They can't help it if their school burned down."

Hindsight being what it is, it's all too easy to predict that not all the other parents would likely share this point of view.

So, while my young imagination was envisioning a gauzy dreamscape vibrant with happy kids stepping off busses as students, parents, and teachers warmly welcomed them into our school, the reality was far from that when the busses pulled up.

"No ni**ers!" the white kids yelled. "Ni**ers go home!"

The kids threw rocks, bottles, and anything else they could find at the busses.

Their parents also screamed and threw things—proving that the proverbial apple does not fall far from the tree.

Hate electrified the air as white families screamed at the busloads of Black children.

I stood close to my mother, a safe distance from the chaos.

Glass bottles rolled and shattered on cement.

Rocks and debris flew.

The school bus doors opened.

A Black boy wearing glasses came down the steps.

He was 11 or 12 years old, and his confused, fearful expression mirrored my feelings.

A rock hit him square in the face, breaking his glasses.

Blood ran down his face. He started crying.

I burst into tears, too.

My mother rushed me across the street to the A&W restaurant at the corner of Fenkell and Meyers. She wanted to get me away from the viciousness and potential danger that was brewing. Plus, nobody was permitted into the school during the chaos.

It was 7:45 a.m., and I distinctly remember ordering a root beer and a chili dog, staring out the window and watching all hell break loose at my school.

Something in that moment changed me. It jolted something too deep within me to understand as a kid. I simply knew that I was witnessing something terribly wrong, and I wanted to someday make a positive difference for people.

As I watched the mayhem on a morning when I should have been in a classroom, I was getting a graphic lesson on racial hatred.

The violence didn't frighten me, because it was commonplace at home. Sadly, by that time, I had done what all kids do in an abusive household: normalize it.

But today marked my first close-up view of bigotry and racism. I didn't understand it. And I knew on some deep and visceral level that it was wrong.

I would later learn that, at the time, Detroit had been enjoying years of prosperity and success. In fact, thanks to the fortunes generated by the booming automotive industry, the Motor City was still known as the Emerald City.

At the same time, the magic of Motown Records was electrifying the national music scene as The Supremes and The Temptations burst onto the radio airwaves and stages across America.

Yet all that wealth and wonder was worlds away from the racial inequities and tensions that had been burgeoning in poorer communities, like the one where I lived. In fact, many people in the city and suburbs were oblivious to it.

Soon, the world would know all about it. Because what I had just witnessed was a flicker of the simmering tension that would explode seven years later during the deadly 1967 riots. The insurrection would cleave a profound racial divide, cause economic collapse and a spike in crime, leave lasting devastation, and ultimately change the trajectory of a city whose crimes and conflicts I would later expose on the airwaves.

DIALING IN ON THE FUTURE

During the 1960s and 1970s, sportscaster Dave Diles on WXYZ AM 1270 had a show that was the precursor of today's sports talk radio, and I didn't miss a single episode.

I loved that he invited listeners to "Dial Dave Diles" and try to stump him with questions. I called many times per week in an attempt to reach him. I was pretty confident in my knowledge of sports trivia, thanks to my older brother Tony, who loved and knew football. He was nearly 10 years my senior, and when he talked sports, I listened.

I also took in every word that legendary Tigers broadcaster Ernie Harwell spoke. The excitement of sports provided a soothing refuge from the chaotic violence of our household. At night, I would crawl under the covers with my powder blue, nine-volt transistor radio and listen to games, whether they were played locally or on the West Coast. As I fell asleep to these games, I absorbed the information like a sponge.

At the same time, I read the sports sections of the newspapers from the first page to the back page.

All of this gave me the ability to stump Dave and go toe-to-toe with him, even though I was just a young kid. As a result, they always put me on the air—which, by my estimation, made me something of a radio personality. And in a way, I was. Dave made jokes about me and called me "Morty in the Morning." The more he joked, the more

I loved him. I frequently sent him letters about how much I longed to be in the business someday.

"Hey, Morty in the Morning," Dave asked one day, "can your dad bring you to the station for a visit?"

My dad agreed, although grudgingly. When we arrived at the station, I was scared.

"Dad, will you come in with me?" I asked.

"I'm staying in the car," he said unceremoniously, and sent me on my way.

So I walked into the station, feeling smaller than my 12 years led me to believe I was. Dave's producer, Sam Adelson, immediately greeted me.

"Dave wants to meet you," he said. "You can sit in the studio and watch and listen. But do *not* talk unless he talks to you."

I nodded vigorously. With hands sweating and heart pounding, I was about to meet my idol. And he was going to interview me! Why else would he want me in the studio with him? I sat quietly and waited. For two hours.

Dave's quizzical look suggested surprise that I was only 12. As he flashed his notoriously wry smile, I was convinced that Dave would toss me on the air, or at least mock my name, just like when I called every night.

But it quickly became clear that he wasn't going to interview me. Instead, I figured out that he just wanted me to sit and listen. And it didn't matter. Dave let me soak everything in, and fall more deeply in love with the idea of being a broadcaster. (Plus, I needed a second career choice, in case being a Major League baseball player didn't work out.)

While sports call-in shows were pretty tame back then, I loved learning all about sports journalism. And it didn't take long to realize that as a journalist of any kind, I could someday inform, shine a light, and impact change. This was my first taste of broadcasting, and like a child to ice cream, I was hooked!

I never forgot the amazing opportunity that Dave had made a reality. Over the years, I continued calling in and writing letters to him. He almost always responded, encouraging me to follow my dream of becoming a sportscaster.

"There is no short-cut to your dreams," he said. "Just make sure you pick a good university to make them happen, though."

I hoped that someday, our paths would cross again. And they would. But not for another 14 years.

Obviously, I didn't become a sportscaster. The news business and an inherent desire to exact change in a less than perfect world had a stronger pull for me. Even so, I didn't make a beeline there. Instead, I veered toward the music business which, depending on the day, was a step up, down, or even sideways. Whatever the case, the wild and unpredictable nature of the music business would certainly prep me for the crazy world of broadcasting. Though truth be told, I was already well versed in navigating my way around the wild and unpredictable.

It had been a necessary skill I'd developed to survive the blustering loose cannon that was my father.

PLENTY OF CRAZY TO GO AROUND

A few months after Black students were met with hatred at my school, four angry white teenagers attacked my mother while she was walking me home.

"Kikes!" they shouted.

They stole her purse, knocked her to the ground, and kicked her.

"Stop!" I screamed at these guys who lived in the neighborhood and knew we were Jewish.

Only seven years old, I had no idea how to protect her. All I could do was stand there and cry. "Please stop! Leave my mom alone!"

Suddenly, my brother Tony showed up. Nine years and nine months older than me, he was a strong and stocky football player. He came at all four of them in a rage that scared them off.

I'll never forget my mother sitting on the ground, bleeding, with her broken glasses hanging down her face. Our next-door neighbors came out to check on her.

Although white residents would say that Detroit experienced its glory days during the 1950s and early 1960s, the neighborhoods where I grew up were far from glorious. Even though they were predominantly white, they were not reaping the rewards of post-war prosperity.

And it was becoming ever more clear that racial intolerance bred by the ignorance in those neighborhoods lent itself seamlessly to religious intolerance as well. Hatred toward Black people was incomprehensible to me; they'd done nothing to me or my family. Instead, I began to see the enemy as white "greasers" like those four teenagers who attacked my mother.

Sadly, the dangerous neighborhood had nothing on what I'd come to call the House of Horrors—our home, the place where a child should feel safe.

My parents fought constantly—usually about money—or lack thereof. My father's pride routinely got the best of him.

To say that he was explosive is an understatement. Standing over 6'2" with a weight that fluctuated between 270 and 350 pounds, he didn't mind flexing his brutality in public, either. In fact, he once threatened to beat the shit out of the tuxedo store owner where he needed a rental for a family wedding. The owner had measured his waist and said, "It's a perfect 62."

My dad asked sheepishly, "Do you have that size?"

Unfortunately, he then called out loud to one of his employees to see if they would be able to get a size 62 tuxedo. That embarrassed my father, who was holding the tuxedo shirt. He threw it at the owner and said, "Shove it up your ass, you dirty bastard."

The owner, somewhat confused, said, "You don't like the way I do business? Then get the hell out of the place!"

"You dirty son of a bitch!" he yelled back, then stormed out of the place as I, my mother, and my brother attempted to keep up with him.

At home, he often sulked around the house in a "wife beater" undershirt and torn boxer shorts which barely stayed up. He was quite a sight. Over the years, I developed the ability to know when to lie low and when it was best to just get the hell out of the house for a few hours.

My father was never without a quick and stabbing insult:

"If you had two brains you wouldn't be a halfwit."

"I do more accidentally than you do on purpose."

"Get out of bed before you get callouses on your ass."

These were just a few of his choice sayings. He didn't just talk the talk, though. He walked the walk, too. He actually challenged two shotgun-wielding, hillbilly neighbors when they demanded that one of my best friends ever, Larry Foote, who is Black, "go back where he belonged."

By this time, I was 14 and we lived in the Detroit suburb of Oak Park. I had invited Larry—who lived in neighboring Royal Oak Township—over to hang out. When the neighbors saw him, they pulled out their guns and confronted my dad.

"Get that ni**er out of your house," they threatened.

"Or what?" my dad sneered.

When one of them dared to step closer, he went right up to him and said, "I'll take that fucking gun, shove it up your ass, then beat you over the head with it."

Two or three police cars pulled up. We don't know who called them. And nobody, against all odds, was arrested.

When we went to the beach, my dad wore a sports coat. Because he was a large man with a 64-inch waist, he didn't want to be, in his words, "mistaken for a whale."

Shopping with my dad was also an adventure. Sometimes he purposely damaged display merchandise to get a discount. For instance, he would kick in the side of a TV, then tell the clerk:

"Hey, it's dented. Give me a good deal."

On one occasion, we actually found a TV with a dead spider between the screen and the picture tube. When my dad pointed this out, we got a deep discount. Then, for years to come, every time the TV was on, the spider corpse would shake in the line of view.

On the surface, it may sound like my dad was a wacky eccentric who was never at a loss for words. But he harbored dangerous anger. Perhaps it resulted from resentment that his brother and sister were given opportunities to attend college, but he was not. Or maybe he was just wired that way.

Whatever the case, an annoying phone call could cause him to tear the phone out of the wall and throw it across the room. Then we'd be without a phone until the phone company could come and fix it. He did this with some regularity.

On another occasion when money was very tight, my mother's brother (my Uncle George), who was a big-time fisherman, wanted to help out. So he brought over a trout that he'd caught. It was big and would have fed us well. But once again, my dad put his pitching arm back to work and threw it against the wall.

I don't mean to make light of it, though. My dad's capacity for rage and violence went far beyond throwing phones and fish.

His physical stature and 300-pound bulk made him even more terrifying as he beat me, my mother, and my brother. During one particularly epic battle in the kitchen one night, my father was trying to attack my mother, but my brother was blocking him in the middle. I stood, horrified, just outside the kitchen as the old floors creaked under the ratty rugs. The harsh overhead lighting bounced off the sheen of grease and filth on the counters.

Crying... screaming... fists flying everywhere.

This was the norm. Sometimes my dad threw dishes and silverware to the floor, then yelled at my mother, "Ella! Pick this shit up!"

When Tony grew into a strong and powerful athlete, he did not hesitate to protect our mother. This triggered nearly constant fist fights with our father.

"Get off her!" my brother yelled when our dad pinned our mother to the floor.

"Mind your own goddamn business, or you'll get yours," our dad roared back.

Once, Tony punched my father in the face as he tried to pull him off of my mother. My father head-locked my brother and rammed his head into our obsolete Kelvinator refrigerator.

The best my mother could do was to retaliate with a slap or a scratch to my father's face, which would often draw blood. My dad would then threaten to take her to the Kosher butcher and have her nails hacked off.

As the violence continued to escalate, it wasn't uncommon for me or my mom to be tossed down the stairs by my dad as if we were rag dolls. As the beatings worsened, the apologies followed, again and again.

The violent reality inside our rented duplex on Meyers Road in Northwest Detroit surely permeated the thin walls, because we often heard our drunken neighbor Jack yelling at his elderly mother, Mrs. Klincher, whose first name none of us would ever know. In Jack's defense, the woman was truly evil. She openly called my mother and brother "dirty Jews."

In retaliation, my father and brother burned trash in our alley when the wind blew just right, so the smoke ruined her freshly washed laundry hanging on the clothesline in her adjacent backyard. How ironic that my father and brother came together in rare moments of solidarity to torch garbage and ruin an old woman's clothes.

Speaking of garbage, our house was truly a pit, full of dust, dirt, and cobwebs. Old beds would collapse and things would seemingly break merely by looking at them. Every day was a horror show.

The holidays were especially bad, since they served as a reminder of how poor we were.

My father made very little money working in his various jobs, which included: cab driver; collection man for a mortgage company; and supermarket manager. Meanwhile, when my mother sold her valuable family antiques, an unscrupulous dealer tricked her, paying only $5.00 for a china closet and $2.00 for a family heirloom chair. But we needed the money to pay the mortgage and put food on the table.

My dad was clearly depressed. I see it now. But as a child and teenager, he just seemed crazy and out of control. Even in later years after we left Detroit to live in the suburbs, he sometimes got very dark and headed to the attic. First he pulled down the creaky stairs, then he began to heft his heavy body upon them.

"Where are you going?" I asked.

"I'm going up to the attic to hang myself," he responded. "Do you want to come?"

I always laughed. But it wasn't funny. Making matters worse, my dad sometimes did a complete 180-degree turn and suddenly became affectionate. For example, he might give me his last quarter so I could buy baseball cards. The next day, the craziness would return, reinforcing the idea that it was dangerous to depend on him.

"YOU ARE NOT MY LITTLE BOY. I WISH I NEVER HAD YOU."

One morning when I was in second grade, my mother forgot to wake me up on time.

"Get up, mister. You're late," she said, ushering me out of bed and offering me my coat.

"But I'm still in my pajamas," I said, confused.

"Yep. You should have thought of that before you slept in so long," she said with a scowl. The corners of her mouth were slightly upturned, making her appear even more menacing. "Looks like you'll be wearing them to school."

"Mom, no," I cried.

"Put on your winter coat," she ordered with a cold tone. "Now!"

Still not comfortable with the idea of wearing my pajamas to school, I hesitated. She yanked me close to her and zipped the hood, catching my hair in it. I screamed and cried.

"Mom, stop! You are hurting me!"

Before I knew what was happening, she smacked my face. Her

eyes went dark and glassy.

"I hate you," she growled. "You are not my little boy. I wish I never had you."

So much for getting ready for school.

Sometimes, in contrast to this meanness, my mother seemed sweet. For example, when she bought her two packs of cigarettes every day, she let me have candy. But generally speaking, she was sweeter to strangers than she ever was to me.

Whether my mother was being gentle, absent-minded, crazy, or irrational, her unique form of brutality knew no bounds, though she was never as physically brutal as my father. Like him, she suffered undiagnosed mental illness. I would later learn that as a child during the 1920s, an illness had left her somewhat mentally diminished. You think?

CONSTANT THREAT OF EVICTION LOOMED

As a child I lived with the constant insecurity that we could be kicked out of our home. Twice we were evicted in Detroit. And when we moved to Oak Park, I hoped things would be more secure.

Wrong.

The Oak Park eviction was actually the worst.

It was an unusually warm but wet Thanksgiving morning in 1963—just days after President John F. Kennedy was assassinated—when the bailiff showed up at our door. My mother knew instantly why he was there. After all, this wasn't our first rodeo. At first, she tried to pretend that she had no idea what was happening. But it was clear that the bailiff would have no mercy on her supposed ignorance. So she switched gears.

"Please," she pleaded. "Please, don't do this. Not today. It's Thanksgiving."

My father came to the door.

The bailiff remained undeterred. He just looked through them saying, "I'm just doing my job."

"You dirty son of a bitch!" my father screamed at the bailiff, peppering him with even less savory names. Meanwhile, Tony—who was attending Wayne State University while living at home—decided that laughing would be the most appropriate behavior. This only further enraged my father.

Before I knew what was happening, a group of people "just doing their jobs" were putting all of our furniture and belongings on the front lawn. We were relegated to sitting outside that cold day, eating unheated beanie weenies from the can—a far cry from turkey and cranberry sauce.

This time, the humiliating experience of our stuff piled on the front lawn, announcing to the world that we were being evicted, was worse than prior times, because we had nowhere to go. In the past, my father had always been able to secure the funds before everything was removed. In Oak Park, we weren't so lucky.

Since it was a holiday, we were unable to reach any family members to help us. We had no access to our phone, anyway. So we spent that Thanksgiving eating and sleeping at a neighbor's house, with our belongings out in the rain. A few days later, we secured money from relatives, so we could get back in. Wet furniture and all.

Looking back at my parents' financial ineptitude is deeply disturbing. Their mortgage payment was just $38.00 per month on an 800 square foot home in "cardboard village," which they bought for $6,000 in 1963—and still my parents couldn't afford to pay it.

As a result, those evictions filled me with tremendous shame that still haunts me. To this day, when I get money, I like to spend it because those childhood financial traumas remain imprinted on my mind. I rarely had things. And when I did, they always seemed to get taken away.

So many times, I wanted to leave the homes where I lived with my parents. But I had nowhere else to go. And my life wouldn't get any easier through adolescence.

HIGH SCHOOL COUNSELOR SETS THE COURSE FOR MY CAREER

As I became a teenager in Oak Park, living under the roof with my father continued to be a nightmare. It didn't matter that the roof was in a somewhat safer neighborhood.

Anyhow, in high school I was clumsy and awkward. Especially around girls. I never went to any dances.

Deep shame consumed me when I invited my few friends over, because our house was small and smelled horrible. Sometimes my "buddies" joked about my house with other friends. Their cruelty only worsened my legacy of shame.

As did my academic performance, or lack thereof.

One day in the eleventh grade, I was called to the counselor's office. What had I done? I wasn't sure. I always tried to keep a low profile to avoid attention—a practice I had learned at home.

"Have a seat, Morty," said counselor Lou Chess.

I sat in the dingy, government-issued school chair, glancing out the window and wondering what I'd done. I wanted nothing more than to jump out that window and just run.

"Look," said the counselor. "My job is to give you guidance."

I just nodded.

"So, here's the thing. You're a nice boy, Morty." He paused.

I sat patiently, wondering why I was here. I couldn't imagine that calling students down to the office for being nice was a regular practice.

"You're a nice boy, but I just don't see you amounting to much," he said, glancing down at a pile of papers. I could only assume that at the top of that pile was a sheet that displayed my grades.

He lifted up that sheet to partially conceal his face. "I recommend you go into the military or into a good trade like plumbing, or you could become an electrician," he said, looking at me from over the edge of the paper. This suggestion was beyond laughable—if it weren't so sad—because of my inability to work with my hands. Hell, I had struggled to pass shop class and art.

I didn't know what to say. Yeah, I knew my grades weren't stellar. But did that really mean I had no future? All I could do was nod, then get up and leave. Utterly humiliated.

As I walked home later that day, I felt stupid and ashamed. I was also afraid. I didn't want to tell my parents—partially due to fear of the wrath it would incur from my father. Even worse, I was scared that it would give him more fodder—proof that I was the idiot he always said I was.

I'm not sure what motivated me to tell my parents, but I did. To my surprise, rather than agreeing with the counselor, they were irate. My father nearly exploded. They went to the school the next day and it was ugly. They proceeded to scream choice words at the principal, and demand a new counselor for me.

This was one of the rare occasions when my father's rage worked in my favor. It's also one of the few times I can say I was grateful to him. Because the next day, I was assigned a new counselor. His name was Harry Weberman, and he would be one of the few highlights of my high school tenure. He acknowledged that I didn't have the best grades. But he nevertheless encouraged me to apply to Wayne State or the University of Detroit, then pursue whatever interested me.

That interaction with Mr. Weberman made me realize that I really had believed I was stupid. But I also realized that my grades didn't truly reflect my intelligence. Truth was, the only subjects that really interested me were English and speech. I simply wasn't interested in other topics, and therefore didn't try very hard. But language and speaking made me tick.

This fact, along with Mr. Weberman's words, gave me hope.

Mr. Weberman was truly an amazing man. He challenged me to follow my dream of becoming a journalist—which I did. Fast forward to 2000, when I was scheduled to give a speech about the media to more than 600 people at the Detroit Jewish Community Center. When I spotted Mr. Weberman sitting halfway back in the audience, I decided to spontaneously switch gears.

Staring out over the crowd, I cleared my throat. "I apologize. I know many of you are here to listen to a speech about the media. And I promise you I'll give it some other time. But today, I want to talk about my high school guidance counselor, Mr. Weberman. Please stand up," I said to him.

I then delivered an impromptu, 45-minute speech with questions regarding the ways that Mr. Weberman inspired me and shaped my future. At the end, few dry eyes remained, and I could hardly see the audience through the blur of my own tears.

For years after that, every time I saw Mr. Weberman, I reminded him about what he meant to me. The last time I saw him was a year or so before he died, at a reunion baseball game for Oak Park High School. I asked others to gather around Mr. Weberman, who was in a wheelchair. Choking back tears, I thanked and honored this great educator one last time. My final words were, "Mr. Weberman, you are everything that is right with education."

He thanked me.

THE ROCK 'N' ROLL LIFE

My music career, as it were, started in 1969. My friend Russ Menenberg and his older brother Matt knew a guy in the music business named Steve Glantz, who had also attended Oak Park High School and grew up in the well-to-do part of Oak Park.

Russ and his brother were selling pop and chips at the world-famous Grande Ballroom, which felt magical every time I entered. Located behind a windowless brick façade at Grand River Avenue and Beverly Court on Detroit's west side, concertgoers entered through three or four sets of metal doors. When we pried them open—yes, *pried* them open—an extraordinarily wide set of stairs led up to a gorgeous ballroom that was a mecca for ballroom dancers during the 1930s and 1940s. Opposite the stage, a man sold incense. The pop and chips bar was stage right.

The cavernous space, with its ornate décor and whispers of an enchanting past, always felt special. Even at age 16, I knew who had come through those doors and performed on that stage.

Steve Glantz's father, Gabe, owned the Grande. Russ asked if I was interested in making a few bucks. At the time, I didn't know what the Grande Ballroom was, other than hearing about it once at a cousin's bar mitzvah. But I figured, why not? Having a little extra dough in my pocket sounded good. I couldn't have guessed how much this decision would dictate the trajectory of my future.

During my first night selling Coca-Cola, chips, and popcorn, Sly and the Family Stone were playing, along with Teagarden and Van Winkle, the Psychedelic Stooges and the Fugs. Concert-goers paid $4 to enter. We earned $18 per night, so to make more money, we picked used cups off the floor and resold them. Then at the end of the night, we tallied our earnings, and split the cash.

Eventually I graduated from selling soda to selling tickets. Meanwhile, I was getting seriously schooled on musicians' eccentricities. One night, Iggy Pop got scantily clothed and romped around the audience.

Another night, Carl Palmer—drummer for Atomic Rooster and later of Emerson, Lake and Palmer—got an encore. Though Carl Palmer would become one of the greatest drummers in rock 'n' roll history, that night Atomic Rooster was the opening act for The Crazy World of Arthur Brown. And opening acts didn't take encores. So when Palmer did, Arthur Brown stormed over to Palmer, yanked him off his drum kit, and started beating him. Palmer was so shocked, he could barely fight back. The whole episode probably only lasted a minute before the stage managers broke it up. But it was so surreal and strange, it seemed to go on forever.

Then, what I'll call the "incident" happened with The Who. Back then, tickets were sold either the night of the show at the box office, or at two major department stores: Grinnell's or J.L. Hudson's. The night we had The Who, Gabe Glantz—owner of the Grande—told the ticket-taker not to rip the tickets, so they could be resold. This made it appear that the band didn't get as many people as they truly did, and Glantz wouldn't have to pay their bonus money. While we're still unsure about how he was caught, The Who's manager found out and threatened not to go on stage that night. They didn't want to disappoint their fans though, so they performed.

Eventually, the Grande closed. The place was rodent-infested, the building was falling apart, and the neighborhood was failing. Plus,

Steve Glantz had a bad reputation because of his father.

MOVING ACROSS TOWN

We moved to The Eastown, a once-glamorous movie house that became a rock concert hall on Harper Avenue on Detroit's east side. We partnered with Bob Begaris, whose company was called Revolution Enterprises. Imagine trying to cash a check with that name at your local bank during the early 1970s, amidst the Black Power Movement and Vietnam War protests.

The Eastown landed equally big names as the Grande, and even more drugs. As bad as drugs were at the Grande, what we saw at the Eastown made the Grande look like a church picnic.

The place reeked of weed; a contact high was guaranteed for anyone who entered. And you couldn't walk 30 feet without someone offering you "reds" or "yellows," heroin, or weed.

The usual drug dealers—Freaky Larry, Crazy Mary, Teddy, Enio, Phyllis, and Downer Debbie—stood hawking their offerings in competition with one another.

"Reds, yellows, got some great smack," Downer Debbie, who sold downers, called out.

"You want some 'shrooms, man?" Teddy offered.

Meanwhile, his buddy Enio called out, "Uppers!"

The drug den atmosphere at The Eastown was no secret around town.

In fact, its notoriety prompted Lou Gordon—a syndicated talk show host from WKBD Channel 50 in Detroit—to try to get The Eastown shut down. So one night he came to do a story, hoping to get footage of the usual brawls, fights and drug deals. But he showed up in an ostentatious limousine, wearing a tacky suit and funny-nose glasses that made him look like Groucho Marx. Not the greatest investigative reporter. And he obviously failed to shut down The Eastown.

However, open drug use would eventually cause the demise of The Eastown.

At any rate, one night while walking in the hallways of the upper balconies, I saw a guy lying unconscious with a needle hanging out of his arm. I was 18 or 19, and had been promoted to an assistant manager-type position. So I called an ambulance, and paramedics took him away. I never knew what happened to that guy, or the many others who came after him.

The interesting thing about the drug scene was that it suddenly made me popular at Oak Park High School. Or at least approachable. Particularly with the kids who wanted drugs or wanted me to book their band. (Or both.) I was never a popular guy. My popularity waned soon enough, though. Drugs weren't really my thing. And no band wanted to hear they weren't good enough to make the cut. It didn't really bother me, however. I was too busy booking shows and traveling around the country.

By the time I was a freshman in college, I drove a 1967 Camaro convertible that I parked at the local Cunningham's, a major drug store chain. It was top of the line—if top of the line meant loaded with a scotch-taped 8-track player that any one-year-old could easily remove. I'd gotten it from one of the neighborhood punks who would come by and sell us tape decks they'd stolen.

One night, one of those kids tried to sell me *my* 8-track player that he'd just stolen. I brought him into the office, slammed him up against the wall, and took my tape deck back. In hindsight, that was not the smartest move. I risked my life and a lot of money over a deck I had bought already stolen. But that's how things were at The Eastown.

As we were getting bigger and bigger and making more money, Steve Glantz established Steve Glantz Productions. The company acquired several nice cars. Sometimes Steve let me use the company's Silver Cloud Rolls Royce, which I drove to school and around campus at the University of Detroit. You can bet I got a lot of attention—from men and women alike. This didn't last long, though. When I asked my friend Nelson Burg, who worked for us, to put oil in it, he poured it into the transmission fluid receptacle. The Rolls stopped rolling. Steve blew up and yelled at Nelson, but he didn't punish us. In fact, he realized that he probably should have blamed himself.

ROCK 'N' ROLL MOMENTS

I remember virtually every show at The Eastown. But one that sticks with me in particular was Leslie West—one of two lead singers for Mountain. The group was popular at that time for their song *Mississippi Queen*. But what made West so memorable was that he was a rare breed. Weighing in at 350 pounds, he was an obese Jewish rockstar with flowing curly hair and a black leather jacket. And he embraced the rockstar persona. After the show, around 2:00 or 3:00 a.m., we went to the Clock restaurant on Harper Avenue, which was Detroit's far east side. The locals, who'd presumably never seen an obese Jewish rockstar, mocked him and made fun of him.

"What the hell are you doing here?" they asked.

West looked at those who were gawking at him and then proceeded to crawl up on a table, stood up, bent over and you can imagine the rest. The ruckus his actions caused resulted in the restaurant almost spinning out of control.

Not many people know that the Joe Cocker and Mad Dogs and Englishmen tour started in Detroit and lasted only a month. While they were practicing in Detroit for their upcoming tour, Bob Begaris and Steve Glantz decided we would do two shows each night for two nights, at $5.00 per ticket. Joe Cocker was huge at the time. The

Eastown, on the other hand, was not huge. It held 1,700 people. At least, legally. But because Glantz and Begaris would pay off the cops and fire department (often with cigarettes), we regularly packed 4,000 to 5,000 people into the place.

The backstage scene of the first show on that first night was like an old-school carnival freak show featuring fat ladies, geeks, and midgets. What made it so strange is that this was rock 'n' roll. While anything goes, this was beyond the pale. Cocker, Leon Russell, Rita Coolidge, and Claudia Lennear (who had a long-time thing with Rolling Stones frontman Mick Jagger) were performing with a cascade of world-class musicians while these "weirdos" danced, drank, and got high.

What was playing out on the stage was even better. It was so great, in fact, that the people from the first show on the first night wouldn't leave when it came time for the second show. When asked to exit, they threw things on the stage. An all-out riot erupted as people swung chairs, hit each other, and threw bottles. People were bleeding. The chaos and violence sent me hiding in the office; despite my familiarity with conflict, I admit having little tolerance for it.

Several hours later, the ushers and security for the first show had finally cleared out the raucous crowd to make space for the second show. The mayhem prompted us to cancel the second show scheduled for the following night. This, of course, caused another fight, because the people who showed up for the second show arrived and became furious that the show was canceled. Unfortunately, The Eastown didn't have the capacity to refund tickets, so the second show hopefuls had to go to Hudson's for their refunds. Their complaints led to some bad press over the whole incident. But the show was still fantastic.

Then came the great Chuck Berry. Now, whatever your opinion of Chuck Berry, I'm here to tell you, he was a perverted and villainous guy. This was a man who was caught in his hometown of Wentzville,

Missouri drilling holes in the bathroom of his house so he could get aroused watching women use the bathroom. And that's just for starters. You never knew what you'd get with Chuck Berry. But performance aside, it usually wasn't good.

In the early 1970s, we brought him to The Eastown. I was the emcee that night. The energy from the audience was pretty amped up. I stepped out on the stage and announced him, "Rock 'n' roll legend, Chuck Berry!" But of course, he didn't come out. So I was standing there looking like a schmuck, waiting for this asshole to come out and perform. A murmur, then a louder protest, went across the audience. I left the stage and went back to his dressing room. I knocked on the door and opened it. And there in plain sight, he was "getting busy" with blonde twins. I glanced to the side with revulsion and said, "Come on, man. We have a show to do here! Let's go!" Then I turned back to look him in the eye.

He gave me a lecherous smile and said, "Let me finish up here."

There's no game book for this kind of situation. So what else could I do except honor his request to let him finish? When he was done, he came out and did a one-hour show like nothing had happened. And I daresay for the twins, nothing probably did.

Then there was Alice Cooper. Born Vincent Damon Furnier, he would be pivotal in bringing horror imagery to rock 'n' roll. And his more than macabre showmanship would transform the genre. It would later be reflected in the equally dark and grim "anything goes" attire of his fans.

When Cooper first started playing the Grande, The Eastown, or the Palladium in Birmingham, Michigan, he'd pull in 1,500 to 1,800 people. In other words, he wasn't a big draw. But then came the song *I'm Eighteen*. It was getting great airplay on WABX—the second major rock 'n' roll FM station in the country—as well as CKLW, a 50,000-watt rocker located across the Detroit River in Canada.

This began his meteoric rise to fame. And it was meteoric. He went from being relatively unknown, to inspiring folks to line up for blocks to see the show. The funny thing is, most people hadn't yet heard of Alice Cooper, and most didn't know about his antics on stage. For instance, he simulated deaths by hanging or electric chair. Or he threw live chickens (and sometimes dead chickens) into the audience. With Alice Cooper, anything could happen. But many of the people who initially liked his music, didn't know any of this. They just knew they liked that song.

As a result, he quickly established a serious fan base. Once, when we went to The Clock restaurant in Southfield, Michigan after the show, Alice Cooper fans were there—with feathers in their hair from the chickens he threw. Strangely enough, for all of his wild stage presence, Alice Cooper wasn't particularly out there. In fact, he was pretty down to earth. He was a good golfer. But he was an even better businessman and a great guy.

At the other end of the spectrum for musicians personalities was Harry Chapin, one of the nicest guys I'd ever met. Certainly, one of the most generous and easy-going musicians.

But I wasn't all that familiar with his music. I saw Chapin as a folksy, hippy type. His relaxed look—with a lambskin coat and wool collar—was different from the rock 'n' rollers we normally booked. Still, something about his music moved me. Chapin was best known at this time for his first major hit, *Taxi*.

"Incredible show," I told him after a show. "I'm more of a rock 'n' roll guy, but it was really good."

"Thanks," he said with a quizzical look. "I think? Do you have any of my albums?"

"No."

"Give me your address," he said. "I'll send you my entire catalog."

In an amusing twist of irony, I took my parents to see Chapin that night. After the show, my father scolded me with his big fat finger and said, "Don't ever take me to hear that juvenile delinquent again. How dare he talk that way." Harry had used the term "motherfucker." While my father was a consummate fan of profanity, that one was beyond the pale for him. Who'd have guessed?

Several weeks later, I received all four of Harry's albums via UPS. No musician had ever done this for me; it engendered great respect for him. And it prompted me to expand my focus beyond rock 'n' roll, and I began to follow him in the trade publications. Time and again, he proved to be an incredibly charitable person. In many ways, it was Chapin who pioneered the concept of playing for free and donating money. We kept in touch over the years, and was devastated when he was killed in a traffic accident in July of 1981 at age 38.

At The Eastown, we promoted other non-rock 'n' rollers, including Paul Anka, whom we also promoted at the Michigan Palace and Masonic Temple; and Vikki Carr, whom we promoted at Masonic Temple. One night, while Vikki Carr was singing, she broke down and started crying. The audience was not sympathetic. Some thought it was a silly stunt and were not amused. And those who realized it was not a stunt felt it was unprofessional. This only made her feel worse.

After the show, she explained to me that she'd just gone through a really rough breakup. She then asked if I'd have dinner with her. At the time, she was 35—which I viewed as "old." After all, I was only 20. But I didn't care about her age. I was excited about the possibility of getting lucky. Because, like I said, I was 20.

So we slowly walked a few blocks to Forbidden City, an iconic Chinese restaurant at the Seville Hotel in Detroit's Chinatown. Or at least, what was left of Chinatown by then. It was clear by the time we finished our egg rolls that nothing romantic would be happening between us. Vikki explained that she was embarrassed and that she'd never broken down on stage before—no matter how bad things were.

But something about this breakup broke her heart. She was sad and just needed someone to listen. And I was that someone.

Vikki Carr turned out to be one of the nicest people I'd ever met in the business. After leaving the restaurant, we shared a cab. And when the cab driver pulled up in front of her hotel, she asked the cab driver how much it would cost to take me home, then gave him the extra money. She exited the cab and entered the hotel. I went home. Alone. Ugh, the story of my life to that point.

MOVING ON TO THE MICHIGAN PALACE

Although it's now an indoor parking lot at Grand River and Bagley in downtown Detroit, the Michigan Palace was once a seriously happening venue between 1973 and 1976. It's strange to think of it now.

The grand opening show in September of 1973 was remarkable, featuring David Johansen's New York Dolls. They were a precursor to Kiss, the Tubes and many groups like them who owe their later popularity to this revolutionary band. It was total glam rock—a British trend featuring wild make-up, glitter, and costumes—and I wasn't sure it was gonna fly. But it blew up.

And they blew away everyone who saw them for the first time. Including me. It was astonishing. Opening for them was a group called Berth, with a then little-known group called Aerosmith, fronted by the now legendary Steven Tyler as the middle group.

Of course, we wound up later booking Aerosmith for many shows. Their managers, David Krebs and Steve Leber, booked them one week at the Michigan Palace, then the next at an ice arena. That sort of classic rock was still somewhat in its infancy in terms of live shows, so managers were doing everything they could to squeeze every drop of money out of the acts that they managed. I always felt this diminished the group, but managers and the bands themselves felt that money was money.

Anyhow, on stage, Aerosmith was a hot group. Off stage, they were more of a hot mess. They fought a lot and it wasn't uncommon for them to show up to perform—appearing to be bombed out of their minds. If you'd asked me back then how long they'd be around, I would have said not very long. Funny how life works sometimes.

Also in 1973, we had Bachman Turner Overdrive opening for Spirit. Spirit could always draw 3,000 to 4,000 people and became a regular at the Michigan Palace. All of this exposure was great for Spirit, which was led by Randy California and his stepfather, Ed Cassidy. It was a weird dynamic and an anomaly that this major band from the West Coast performed together successfully for so many years. In fact, Cassidy played with California until he was 80 years old.

Anyhow, California grew up playing guitar with Jimi Hendrix and had a number of FM hits and a few AM hits. He was a real character. In his 20s and 30s, he always had a thing for older women in their 50s and 60s. Another oddity was his habit of picking up street people before he performed during sound check, giving them a hit of acid or mescaline and hanging out with them for a while. They were usually older women in their 40s and 50s, so you can figure out what he was doing with them. Then he went on stage and performed.

Like many rockers, Randy California was plagued by drug and alcohol problems. But by the 1990s, he had cleaned up and was in recovery. Sadly and tragically, he later drowned in the ocean while saving his son from drowning.

"SIX OF THE GREATEST NIGHTS OF MY LIFE"

The fall of 1973 brought six of the greatest nights of my life: when David Bowie planned the Michigan Palace from October 15 to the 20th. Even though he was already legendary at this point, and could have easily filled the larger Cobo Arena downtown Detroit, he still preferred smaller venues. And since he was something of a fashionista and closely bound with the fashion world, the audience was its own bizarre and fascinating costume show.

Women came to see Bowie decked out in sophisticated but hot dresses that were often transparent. And some men showed up in costumes that were almost always a failed attempt to look like Bowie himself. Looking back, it felt very like big time theater. In many cases, it was the Theater of the Absurd.

Coming face-to-face with Bowie was a unique experience. He was unapproachable—both figuratively and literally.

"Don't make direct eye contact with him," his manager told me. "And definitely do not try to strike up a conversation with him unless he initiates it."

Hell, I didn't need to be told that! If I were ever intimidated and smitten with true rock royalty, this was the occasion.

Each night I'd sit in Bowie's dressing room with a bunch of people—his wife, manager, members of the band, and others. Even though additional dressing rooms were available, people always wanted to be around him. When Bowie did talk in that dressing room, his words were measured and his voice was soft. You never knew what to expect from Bowie, though, and he could turn on a dime. One night he'd go out in a tuxedo, another night a leotard. He didn't talk much, either. So even though people were always around him, they were generally talking to each other.

Back then, audience behavior could be pretty poor. Opening night, someone threw a tomato. It nearly hit his wife. He stopped the show and walked off the stage for quite some time.

I hold David Bowie in the highest esteem. There was never anyone like Bowie before and probably never will be again. He had the stage presence, the performance, the passion, the theatrics, the lyrics. He had it all. He was enigmatic, electrifying, and mesmerizing. To this day, I see him as the Frank Sinatra of rock 'n' roll.

During the time that Bowie was at the Michigan Palace, I heard about a little-known group called KISS playing over in Windsor, which is just across the Detroit River in Ontario, Canada. I went to check them out after their New York agent asked me to go take a look. They were certainly a spectacle—wearing thick, full-face Halloween/horror makeup, and black leather outfits highlighted with metal studs and even space-age silver metallic, all while running around on six-inch, platform heels. The rockers became notorious for their regalia, and the fans loved it.

When members Paul Stanley, Gene Simmons, Peter Criss, and Ace Frehley heard I was with The Michigan Palace, they asked if I could get them into the theater to see Bowie. Even though we had Bowie for six nights, two shows each night, Bowie's management contract explicitly prohibited comps and guest lists. But I wanted to cut these guys a break. So I snuck them up the fire escape, officially marking their first time at The Michigan Palace.

KISS made their Michigan Palace debut six months later, on Sunday, April 7, 1974. Oddly, after headlining that day, they opened for Blue Oyster Cult five days later.

It's no secret that the members of KISS were never great musicians. But for whatever reason, the band became an overnight success. They eventually performed *Kiss Alive!* at Detroit's Cobo Hall, and I was the emcee who brought them on stage. I'll never forget that night. The crowd was wild! Their popularity blew my mind. But despite their horror show image, they were nice guys and really easy to get along with. Even Gene Simmons, who was famous for flicking his tongue.

In September of 1975, I received a phone call from either the athletic director or high school football coach of the Cadillac High School Vikings in Cadillac, Michigan. Could I, they asked, bring KISS to their northern Michigan town the following month to play a homecoming concert in their gym? Pictures and video confirmed that

KISS accepted the invitation and made the show happen. Not since The Who played Southfield High School in suburban Detroit during the mid 1960s had I heard of such a thing. KISS revisited the school and posed for a photo with a giant granite statue dedicated to their appearance. This story remains a cornerstone in KISS's storied career.

During the 1990s, KISS gave me a gift that they'd intended to deliver decades earlier: a framed Platinum album of *KISS: Alive*, recorded live at Cobo Arena in Detroit.

BURNING DOWN THE HOUSE

On February 22, 1974, I thought the Michigan Palace was going to burn down. Literally. Up to this point, we'd never done a "Black" show. But that night, the Ohio Players were there. And so were their fans—which consisted primarily of white kids. At this point, the band already had three or four major hits with a number of crossover hits.

So here are these guys in their crazy green suits who were probably too stoned to cross the street, let alone go on stage. Then when they started playing their tune *Fire*, they encouraged the audience to "Light any motherfucking thing you have!" In a matter of seconds, potato chips bags, popcorn boxes, hotdog sleeves—you name it—everything was going up in flames.

The fire marshals stepped in, threatening to shut down the show. It was terrifying. I truly feared the building would be nothing more than cinders by the end of the night. Some people did suffer minor burns. But the show went on and it was a success, in spite of, or perhaps because of, their antics.

Another memorable night occurred when Sly and the Family Stone were scheduled to perform on November 14, 1974. I had a special place in my heart for them, since they had played on my very first night back at the Grande. Well that, and they were just fantastic. Anyhow, on this night, the Chambers Brothers were the opening act.

While they played, I drove the company Rolls Royce to pick up Sly and his band mates from the airport. While standing at the gate, anxiously awaiting their arrival, I first saw Sly's father, Reverend Stewart, in all his glory. Then came Larry Graham, Sister Rose, Cynthia, and Freddie. But no Sly. Finally, when it seemed everyone was there, I asked, "Where's Sly?"

"Oh," Reverend Stewart began, "he be in Chicago. He missed his flight."

And that was that. So I had to go on stage and announce that Sly and the Family Stone would be missing Sly. Of course, as the messenger, I knew I'd be shot. The audience booed and threw stuff at me. Sly caught a later plane and eventually showed up, taking the stage at around midnight. He did a show for the ages. But I'd learned that this was just the way with Sly. Sometimes he'd show, sometimes he show up late, and sometimes he wouldn't show up at all.

When he was on though, he was on.

Another act was Bob Seger, who played two nights in April of 1975. He sold out both shows. This might not come as a surprise. But at that time, he didn't have any major commercial hits yet. At this point, Seger was doing songs like *Lucifer* and *Back in '72*. It would be another year before *Live Bullet* and *Beautiful Loser* came out. It was also before the Silver Bullet Band.

Meanwhile, we also featured non-musical acts, including comedian George Carlin in 1975. To be honest, Carlin was a miserable prick until we smoked a joint or two. And something of a thief, too.

On the night of his show, we were talking backstage. I had wanted to show him a trick lightbulb that would go on and off in your hand. I made a joke that piggybacked off the Ford commercial that used the lightbulb.

George just looked at me deadpan and asked me to give him the lightbulb. I did, of course. Then when he went out on stage—and he used my joke! The audience of 5,000 laughed. And did I get a thanks or even a nod?

You can probably guess the answer to that one.

BRUCE SPRINGSTEEN BECOMES MY NEW HERO

My rock 'n' roll life as I knew it changed forever on September 23, 1975. I was sitting with Steve Glantz in his basement "office" at the Northfield Condominiums in the Detroit suburb of Troy, because it was also where Glantz happened to live.

Anyhow, the phone rang early that afternoon. It was Punch Andrews, who goes by Punchy. He was, and still is, Bob Seger's manager. Punch has managed this music legend brilliantly over the years, creating one of the most successful acts in rock 'n' roll history. Bob Seger has been around since the mid-1960s, and he can still sell out major arenas, even though, as of this writing, he is in yet another retirement.

So, back in September of 1975, when I answered the phone, his manager said, "Morty? Punchy."

I didn't even have a chance to say anything before he continued.

"Listen, Bobby and I are going to Hill Auditorium in Ann Arbor tonight to see a guy. Bruce Spring-something or other. We've got a couple of extra tickets. You wanna go?"

I didn't have much going on, so I figured, what the hell? This was just weeks before Springsteen landed the covers of *Time* and *Newsweek*. But I'd heard about him. I was at least familiar with the name. So I figured I would take a chance. I called up my boyhood pal Bernie Fassberg, who also happened to have nothing going on and we headed to Ann Arbor.

When we arrived at Hill, Punch was out front waiting for us. He handed us two tickets for the sixth row. Their tickets were for the seventh row. I started getting really amped. Once we got to our seats, I turned around to Punch and Seger and said, "This is probably the only time I'll ever be closer to the stage than you guys!" I was 22, but felt like a young teenager—sitting there, front and center, waiting for this Bruce Springsteen guy to come out on stage. I had no idea what to expect. And before I knew it, there he was, playing *Incident on 57th Street.* He went through his array of songs—none of which I'd heard—including *Born to Run.*

Hearing them that night changed my life.

I was taken. I couldn't quite put my finger on what swept over me that night. But I knew I wanted to bring Bruce to the Michigan Palace. So after the show that night, I went backstage and met Mike Appel, who was his manager at the time.

"We run the Michigan Palace, and I think Bruce would be a great fit for us," I said. The next Monday, we talked to Premier Talent in New York about booking him. And two weeks later, he played at the Palace.

During the Springsteen promotions at the Michigan Palace, we seated about 4,000 people. I think we only sold 3,000 tickets—because we only had a two-week window to sell tickets.

Springsteen was a good guy right out of the gate. The audience's enjoyment has long been his priority. In fact, a few years later in 1978 while performing New Year's Eve in Cleveland, someone threw a firecracker on stage.

"That fucking shit could have hurt someone... blown someone's eye out," Bruce said, later recalling that moment. But instead of getting angry or upset, he spit on the stage, looked down, then faced the audience.

"It's not gonna ruin my New Year's Eve, and I hope it doesn't ruin yours," he said. Then he blasted into a song. He even offered a money-back guarantee if someone wasn't satisfied by the end of the fifth song. I'm not sure if anyone ever took him up on that. It's not something I'd have ever considered.

I emceed the show that night. And it was magic. The bootleg is still out there for all to hear.

After the performance, but before his encore, I was sitting on the backstage steps leading to his dressing room. When he came off stage, I said, "Man, you are a superstar."

He looked at me, glanced down, spit on the floor, and said, "Thanks, man." Then he returned to the stage and did his encore, *Born to Run.*

Listening to him perform, I felt profoundly different. I can't really explain it. I thought, *This guy is like Bob Dylan. But different. More upbeat. More spiritual, maybe?*

The way I interpreted his songs resonated with something deep inside me. He ran sentences and words together which I didn't understand, but I had no need to understand. He got me. And from that night forward, Sly and the Family Stone—previously my favorite band—took second billing.

After the show, I was hanging out backstage with Bruce and the rest of the band. He said he was hungry. We had our usual catered food, but it was clear that particular brand of "cuisine" wasn't going to do the trick. We wanted Bruce to have the full Detroit experience.

"Let's go to Lindell AC," Glantz said. The well-known Detroit sports bar just down the street had seen many celebrities, and even more fights. Bruce was all for it. So we got in the limo and headed there. On the way, Bruce decided he wanted to stand on the hood. So there we were, driving along Bagley Avenue through downtown Detroit shortly after midnight on that warm night with the inimitable Bruce Springsteen standing on the hood of the car like a hood ornament. It was an unforgettable night. And I didn't realize it was the start of something incredible in my life.

My friend Nelson was as taken by Bruce as I was, and we became Springsteen groupies, so to speak. On one occasion, Nelson and I traveled to Asbury Park, New Jersey, to hopefully catch Bruce slumming at the famous Stone Pony. We showed up looking for him at his house in a nearby city, but no luck. So we decided to do the next best thing—find out where sax man extraordinaire Clarence Clemons (a.k.a. The Big Man) lived. With the help of the mayor of Seabright, we found his house.

I knocked on his door and a *zaftig*—that's Yiddish for plump—woman with blonde hair greeted Nelson and me.

"Good afternoon, ma'am," I said politely.

She smiled.

"We were wondering if Clarence was home?" It felt a little like being a kid and asking if Clarence could come out and play. Which to some extent, was what we were asking.

She just looked straight at us and yelled, "Clarence, there are some boys here to see you, what should I do?"

The Big Man came to the door, wearing shorts and a bright red T-shirt. This guy was bigger than life. We talked for a bit and told him we'd been at the Stone Pony looking for Bruce.

"Any idea where he might be?" Nelson asked.

Clarence nodded. "Couldn't tell you where he is right now. But I suspect that Bruce and some of the guys will be there one of the next four nights. No promises or guarantees, you understand."

Since the purpose of our time in Asbury Park was to essentially stalk Bruce, we just returned to the Stone Pony every night and on the last night, he was there. Bruce treated us like royalty and wanted to know how we were doing and why we were hanging out. We were beyond thrilled to meet him, and furthermore, to hang out with him. Then he proceeded to play there for an hour and a half in what became another life-changing night.

Over the years, from then until now, I've seen Bruce Springsteen 131 times. It seems that in my tormented life—as it's often been—he's always been there as a salve or balm to bring me relief. Even when I had tragedies and losses in my family, I always took solace in listening to Bruce.

While I felt that I'd have an abiding relationship with Bruce and his music, the music business itself was beginning to wear on me. Yes, my experiences at the Grande, Eastown, Michigan Palace, and eventually Cobo Arena and the Pontiac Silverdome—where The Detroit Lions football team played—were valuable.

But I finally quit working with Glantz in 1976 after we booked a show at the Silverdome for Seger. Glantz was supposed to pay him $60,000, but didn't have the funds. He was going to write him a check, knowing it would bounce. That's just not how I do business.

I knew it was time to make the transition to broadcasting.

JUST A PEON

The chaotic freak show that was my childhood had not only prepared me for the music business, but it also provided the unique skill set required to serve as a peon in the world of broadcasting.

The two worlds of rock 'n' roll and journalism overlapped during the years I studied Broadcasting and Journalism at the University of Detroit. While I'd spend evenings immersed in smoke and loud music, my days were spent on this small and quaint campus with archaic buildings that were blackened with soot. The interiors were equally dated. None of this detracted from the amazing education I was getting there.

Academics by day, rock 'n' roll by night. I like to joke that I chose U of D over the larger Wayne State University because it was easier to park. That's partly true. At the end of the day, though, it ended up being a good fit. Yeah, a few terrible teachers carried no shame for being racist and/or anti-Semitic. But I encountered far more good ones. And many of them were inspirational to me.

Being a Jesuit institution, the outside perception was that the instructors were sullen priests and nuns who had no capacity to smile. But nothing could have been further from the truth. In fact, I had one teacher who was an ex-nun who'd left the convent to become a teacher. Margaret Maxey taught subjects like *Death and Dying*, *Sexual Liberation*, and *Changing Man/Woman Relationships*. And this was in the early 1970s. She also threw legendary parties for the students at her apartment… and they were big fun. This was one ex-nun who was very hot.

Those college years were crazy. But it was a good crazy.

That's where my journalism career began: I was the basketball play-by-play guy on the school radio station. This was a big deal, because I was still dreaming of being a sportscaster at this point. One night when the team was playing at the University of Minnesota, I was doing a live, courtside broadcast. The late Terry Thomas—who would later play in the NBA—threw a buzzer-beater shot that would win us the game. Announcing that shot literally brought me out of my seat with a primal scream. People who heard the broadcast were sure I was having a heart attack. I loved it, and dreamed of someday announcing for baseball.

Still, any time I had the option to go on the road for a concert, I went—even if it conflicted with a basketball game or a class. And I was traveling a lot, logging hours on planes and in cars. I was rubbing elbows with Barry Manilow in Cincinnati one night, Rod Stewart the night after in Milwaukee, then Sly and the Family Stone in Chicago two days after that. This gave me status. Girls who never gave me the time of day in high school suddenly wanted to talk to me.

This, and studying broadcast journalism at U of D, made me feel for the first time that my life was normal. Although there weren't many Jews there, I made a lot of friends. Outside of the occasional query from an ignorant person who'd heard urban myths about Jewish people (having horns or a yellow streak down the back), it was a great place. And it's where, perhaps more importantly, I officially fell in love with broadcast journalism and communications.

"KID, YOU'RE A TERRIFIC WRITER… FOLLOW YOUR DREAMS"

Of the many great instructors at U of D, Phil Nye was the biggest motivator for my eventual move to broadcasting. I met him in 1974 as a student in his News Writing for Broadcast class.

"Kid, you're a terrific writer," he told me. "Stick to it, follow your dreams."

So I did.

When I finished college in 1975, Phil was the legendary news director at WXYZ, ABC Channel 7 in Detroit. He'd been a newsman at local AM WKNR—known as Keener 13—and was later credited with being one of the men who started and proliferated "happy talk" with the ABC-owned and operated stations. He was brilliant, well-respected and intimidating enough to manage Detroit TV news anchor legend Bill Bonds. Only a small handful could lay stake to that claim.

Since he'd so wholeheartedly encouraged me to follow my dreams, I started to ask Phil for work. I wrote him letters and called him regularly. Sometimes he responded.

In August of 1976, just before I parted ways with Steve Glantz and what I viewed as his questionable business practices, I wrote Phil a letter and finally got a response. He said he expected a bottom-rung position to open up soon at the station and if I wanted it, it was mine. I of course took this as a free pass to show up at the station three to five days every week and sit outside his office. One day between Christmas of 1976 and New Year's Day of 1977, he walked out of his office, stopped, and sighed. Standing there in his expensive suit, bad toupee, and Gucci shoes and briefcase, he took his glasses off and said,

"Morty? If I hire you, will you leave me the fuck alone?"

Of course, I said, "Yeah."

He nodded quickly, told me to report the following Monday, and walked away.

Over the weekend, my parents took me to Northland Shopping Center in suburban Southfield. We went to the Richman Brothers clothing store, where they bought me a cheap, three-piece suit. I put it on early that Monday morning, and was feeling awesome. I walked into the station lobby and thought of that day so long ago when my father took me to meet Dave Diles, but wouldn't join me inside the station. This wasn't the same place, of course. But I was just as excited. Here I was, 11 years later, and I was finally on my way.

My job—as a production assistant—was a euphemistic title for "grunt." I worked under executive producer Steve Cohen, who would later go on to do big things. Cohen told me he'd teach me the ropes. I thought my job was part-time, but was assigned to work 2:30 to 11:30 p.m., Monday through Friday. And despite it being an interruption to being able to play baseball and attend games and shows, I wasn't about to complain. I was ready to get started.

Back in the late 1970s, news file film was kept in a "film attic" for seven years. My first job in journalism was sorting that film. By the end of the day, my new blue suit was so covered with dust that it had turned grey. But I didn't mind. I was determined to keep a good attitude. It didn't take long, though, before I was confronted by three other production assistants. They cautioned me about my "too good an attitude." They'd been there for four years and told me that PAs never got promoted. Never.

Even Bill Bonds pulled me aside during this time and said, "Kid, what are you doing? Don't become too good at that shit, because then that's all you will ever do. When a ribbon on a typewriter needs to be changed or paper needs to be added to the wire machines, go take a leak. Vomit. Whatever it is, just disappear. Otherwise you will only ever be a gopher."

BILL BONDS—A LARGER-THAN-LIFE LEGEND

A legendary figure in Detroit, Bill Bonds was, by any measurement, one of the five greatest anchormen ever. Anywhere. Period. Bill was bigger than life. Brilliant and tough as nails, it was no secret that he struggled with his (not-so) private life. He'd done more than a dozen stints in rehab for drinking and had lost a daughter to a drunk driver. Bill was passionate about his job—known for challenging Detroit Mayor Coleman Young to a boxing match for charity and ending each newscast with, "Have a peaceful evening."

But he could be snarky and argumentative like nobody's business. After each newscast, Bill would hold up the scripts in the newsroom and ask, "Who wrote this? Who wrote this piece of shit?"

Someone would meekly raise their hand and Bill would stare them down and say, "We are better than this. This is terrible." Then for dramatic effect, he'd sometimes fling the scripts into the air and walk out on his way to dinner or, more likely, the bar. That was just Bill. I loved him. We all loved him.

I didn't allow the words from the production assistants or even Bill to discourage me in those early days, though. Instead, I took it as a challenge. I came in early, stayed late, volunteered to learn, and made the unions mad at me for working overtime for free. But I learned a lot. And I was moved up to weekend assignment editor within four months. My salary, as it were, went from \$104 to \$200 per week.

In the meantime, the station had become too cheap to purchase coffee. But not having coffee was not an option. So a group of us who called ourselves the UGB (Ungrateful Bastards) collected funds to pay for it. One day, Bill Bonds came up to me and asked to borrow five dollars to contribute to the coffee fund. Although it was all I had, I happily gave it to him. It was Bill Bonds, after all.

Despite his huge salary, Bill never did repay that five dollars that he "borrowed" for the coffee fund. But that was partially my doing. Because whenever I'd been on air and people asked me to tell stories about Bill Bonds, I took great joy in telling that story. He actually did agree to pay me back in exchange for no longer telling it. But I refused. I told him I preferred that he always owed me something.

Of course, I'd never be at a loss for stories about Bill Bonds. And not surprisingly, many of the stories aren't as G-rated as that one. During that same era when I was a lowly production assistant, I ran the teleprompter for Bill. Although he had warned me not to get too good at one single job so I wouldn't get stuck doing it forever, I was so good at the teleprompter, that he always wanted me to work it for him.

Anyhow, one summer day, the Howell Michigan Melon Queens were scheduled to appear on the newscast. They were there to promote the Howell Melon Festival, which showcases the Howell melon, a cantaloupe hybrid that is allegedly found only in the area surrounding Howell. And they felt that bikinis were the proper attire to promote this event—which I'm sure drummed up motivation for some people. At any rate, the women were standing off to the side, spilling out of their bikinis, while Bill read the news. The floor manager instructed them to wait until the break to bring the cantaloupes out on the set. They decided not to wait and came out while Bill was reading the news.

Bill looked at one of them and said, "Honey, give me those cantaloupes and you can put those melons down on the desk in front of me," in the middle of the newscast. John Kelly was anchoring with Bill Bonds that night and he and Bill laughed so hard that they had to go to break.

Even though by today's standards this would be considered brazen, cavalier, sexist, and insensitive, this was the late 1970s. And Bill Bonds was notorious for being all of these things. It simply wasn't punishable. But in the case of the Melon Queens, the event did set the precedent to further prohibit scantily clad women in the studio.

Other times, Billy could be amazing.

On the night of January 13th in 1978, Hubert Humphrey died. But by the 11:00 p.m. newscast, the former presidential candidate who had progressive ideas for bridging America's racial divide and worked with President Lyndon B. Johnson to do so, was still clinging to life.

Shortly before eleven, Billy came to my desk and said, "Morty, stand at the fucking wire machine and if Humphrey buys it, let me know. Come down to the studio, no matter what time it is."

So there I was, staring at the gigantic wire machines that printed reports from United Press International and Associated Press.

Right at about 11:20 p.m., 10 bells rang and three words appeared on the wire: "Hubert Humphrey dead."

I took the copy, ran out of the newsroom, down a flight of stairs, up another flight of stairs, and then down another flight of stairs. I got into the studio just as they were about to say goodnight.

Billy said, "Morty Meisner has just walked into the studio. What do you have for us?"

I waved the copy in the air as the floor manager was wrapping Bill. Bill told him to quit wrapping him and that they were running over. Then he invited me to the anchor desk, where I handed him the copy.

"Morty Meisner has just confirmed that Hubert Humphrey has died," he said. And then, as if out of the blue, he recited an amazing and completely unscripted seven-minute obituary. At the end, he leaned into the camera and said, "Goodnight, Happy Warrior." This was Humphrey's nickname.

After the broadcast, we went to Mr. Joe's, a local gin mill, and drank until well after 2:00 a.m. Still amazed at what I saw that night, I said to him, "Billy, that was the best fucking ad lib I have ever seen or heard."

Billy turned his head to look at me and pulled me in close

enough that his mouth was almost on mine. I could smell the alcohol on his breath.

"There are no fucking ad libs," he said.

What he meant was that he'd already committed the Hubert Humphrey obituary to his memory, and had simply let it roll from there.

He was the best ever. Period.

Yet for all of his talent and ability, Billy was often in trouble. In fact, he was suspended by management more times than I can count on two hands. I can't even remember on how many occasions I was told by Phil Nye or Steve Cohen to "pack up Billy's boxes, he's done."

A few times, I delivered those boxes to his house. At $300,000 per year, he was one of the highest paid in the industry at that time. Even so, he always had uncashed checks lying around ($6,000 per week) because everywhere he went, someone else always footed the bill.

In the years that followed, it was not uncommon for many of us from the station to be at Mr. Joe's or the Balloon Saloon in Southfield when Billy would stagger into the bar and ask us to front him money for beer.

It was kind of sad, really.

RISING THROUGH THE RANKS

In the meantime, I continued to plug away at WXYZ and it seemed I was pretty well-liked. In fact, one of my bosses ordered me to date his daughter. He actually ordered me! He didn't like his daughter's boyfriend. So I asked her out and we started dating.

Her parents were divorced, and she lived with her mother and sister. But my boss would occasionally stop over to visit them. One early morning, he dropped in to find his daughter and me in bed together. I froze up in fear, but all he said before he shut the bedroom door behind him was, "Good. Just checking up on you."

Eventually, his daughter went back to the boyfriend, much to my boss's chagrin. And when this boyfriend died in an accident not too much later, he merely said, "Good. Now maybe you can get back with her."

It didn't take me long to recognize that the news world was full of drama. One of my craziest memories at WXYZ was when a well-known reporter who would later rise to CNN called in one morning and said, in his ever-so-distinguished voice, "Mort, I will not be coming in today. I have a bit of a problem."

"Oh," I said. "I hope it's not too major."

"Well," he paused, then said calmly, "it seems that my wife found out about my girlfriend in the apartment upstairs. I suppose it was partially my fault for answering my girlfriend's door when my wife knocked. Of course, I had no idea it was her."

"Oh, boy," was all I could think to say.

He continued. "When I answered the door and saw it was her, I tried to escape back into my girlfriend's apartment. It didn't go well."

"I imagine it didn't. What happened?"

Then he just said in the same very matter-of-fact tone with which he delivered the news, "She stabbed me. In the back. I have a knife in my back."

I gasped at the thought of this reporter with a knife sticking out of his back. Then to make the whole situation all the more surreal, he added, "But don't worry. I'll be back in tomorrow."

You just can't make this stuff up.

EGOS AND PARTIES APLENTY

I would meet a lot of big and blustery people like Bill Bonds in broadcasting. Some were pretty legendary, while others were more legends in their own minds. Either way, they made things interesting. Especially when it came to the historic parties on the lawn.

These extravagant bashes featured hay rides and horse rides and chefs from famous restaurants who came in to cook. And with the constant flow of alcohol and drugs, the festivities quickly escalated into sheer debauchery, with bras and panties showing up in the bushes the next day.

At one such party, I got into a beer drinking match with a Bill Bonds heir apparent who went to Connecticut to establish his career. He and I had a race to see who could guzzle ten, 16-ounce beers faster. Ten. Nobody won, because I can say with certainty that we both lost. I lost my car and had to call the Southfield Police to help me find it. It was an authentic (and authentically embarrassing) "Dude, Where's My Car?" moment. But again, it was a different time. And it's just how the business was.

When Channel 7 hired Jerry Stanecki, it didn't take long before we were all calling him Jerry Stan'Ego. Prior to this, Jerry had made his mark as a mobster/teamster reporter who had the last interview with Jimmy Hoffa, the deposed Teamsters leader who was kidnapped, presumably murdered, and then dumped here, there, and everywhere in July of 1975.

Phil Nye hired Jerry and debuted him as the "Newshawk." This was the 1970s version of *Problem Solvers* wherein the station was made aware of some sort of need or injustice in the city, and Jerry would insert himself to make things right. This guy would take on anything. Truly. And I was his first Hawkette, so to speak.

Depending on how you looked at it, this was either a good or not-so-good thing. If nothing else, it was amusing. One of the first problems I tackled with Jerry was to fulfill the request of some elementary school students who needed taxidermy animals. They were using them for a project of some sort—though we didn't institute our investigative skills to dig a whole lot deeper on what that project was. Jerry was just ready to answer their prayers. Or more accurately, ready for me to answer their prayers. Because I was dispatched to the taxidermists to pick up raccoons, porcupines, skunks, bobcats, and any other number of stuffed creatures. Once I collected the macabre menagerie in the back of my car, I looked it over, shook my head, and questioned why I'd gone to school for this.

But nickname notwithstanding, Jerry really did do things that helped make a difference in people's lives. Dead and stiffened animals aside, he was able to secure a set of replacement eyes for someone who'd never been able to see. And he was there to celebrate the day the person did the equivalent of taking his first steps. So his generosity stretched far.

NEGATIVE GUYS IN THE NEWSROOM

That generosity and good spirit sure as hell didn't extend to Al Ackerman or Bob Page. Al and Bob were two of the most negative guys I'd ever met. By this time, I was running the evening assignment desk during the week. Not only was I in charge of what stories were covered, but I was the traffic cop for the crews getting moved around. Back then, the crew for sporting events was created from the news crew. So I usually made sure they had a crew. But if a big news story was breaking, I'd have to pull the crew.

Al was a curmudgeon in his 50s who, given the chance, would have kicked Mother Teresa in the ass rather than walk around her. Not a nice guy. But as a sportscaster, he was someone who took on the Detroit Lions and the public funding for the Pontiac Silverdome. He also challenged Jim Campbell of the Detroit Tigers, as well as Detroit Lions' General Manager Russ Thomas, who was an admittedly horrible GM.

But if Al felt slighted in any way, let's just say he didn't handle it with aplomb. The day after I had to pull his crew, he chewed me out.

"You dirty mother fucker, you took my crew last night," he seethed. "You're a piece of shit!" he yelled and stormed off.

I wasn't going to take that. So I went into the sports office.

"You need to apologize to me!" I said.

"Fuck off!" he answered.

The guy was so determined to not apologize that he tried to leave, but I blocked the door. So he turned around and tried to crawl out the first-floor window. It came down on his hand and severed a tendon in his middle finger.

Karma? Maybe something like that. Anyhow, he went to the hospital and got stitches. But that, or course, was not the end of it. He felt the need to blame me for his injury. As he was doing a commentary about the Detroit Lions, he held up that bandaged middle finger to Russ Thomas, the GM for the Detroit Lions. He did get suspended for that. But he even tried to blame that on me. He went as far as complaining to management that it was my fault. They knew he was full of hot air—among other things.

As for Bob Page, he ceaselessly chided me for working too hard and "making too many one-handed catches" when we worked together at WXYZ in the late 1970s.

He said I would one day understand that my job was just a job and that I should fill out my timesheet and collect my check. He was also combative and always trying to bait me.

Knowing that I was a U of D basketball fan, he took it upon himself to tell me that two star players on the team—All-Americans Johnny Long and Terry Tyler, known as Thunder and Lightning—would end up going nowhere and probably be shooting heroin in an alley six months after graduating college. Fortunately, he was wrong. Both went on to enjoy great basketball careers in the NBA. Though I suspect this didn't make my colleague any less racially tone deaf.

WORKING ALONGSIDE EXCELLENCE

I worked with Kathryn Kiefer at WXYZ in Detroit and can say that she is the best female reporter with whom I ever worked. Whether on a feature or when we collaborated on a string of rapes and murders in Detroit, she was as good as it gets. She's a great writer who was tough, talented, and street smart.

A stunningly beautiful woman, she was the antithesis of what most reporters looked like in the industry at that time. It was her brilliance and stellar reporting skills over the years, though, that landed her jobs in cities like Chicago, Denver, San Francisco, and Boston. She had, and still has, a serious "don't fuck with me" streak that made her one of the few people, male or female, who could occasionally intimidate me.

One such time this happened was on a weekend in late May of 1977. Dr. Victor Herman, a Russian immigrant who had served time in Siberia, was trying to get his daughters Svetlana and Janna into the United States from Russia via Canada. Finally, it was to happen on a very early morning weekend flight. Kiefer was scheduled to work the weekend and was due in at 5:00 a.m. for the early arrival of these young women.

She stumbled into the studio that morning with sunglasses covering late-night eyes and a scowl that could shrivel a flower.

"Good morning!" I said, nervously.

Kiefer sneered at me and asked, "What the fuck am I doing in here so early to cover some kind of stupid reunion?" She pulled her purse up over her arm with an extra touch of drama. "Come on. You're coming to the bathroom with me so I can put on my face."

"Okay," I said sheepishly.

"And this *better* be a great story," she threatened as we walked into the women's room. Of course, I wasn't foolish enough to ask, "Or what?"

In the end, it did turn out to be a great story. She'll never admit it, though.

Perhaps not as well-known as Bill Bonds around Detroit, Ven Marshall was a great reporter who occasionally sported a big, handlebar mustache. This was a guy who would pull out all the stops and histrionics in the field just to get a story.

For instance, when Federal Department Stores were going out of business, they were laying people off. Owner Steven West was blamed for the 54-store chain's failure because he was allegedly draining profits at his employees' expense.

People were trying to nail him and Ven was hungry to get an interview with the owner. So he made a deal with all the other reporters at the scene on the stake-out. But nothing was happening.

So Ven said, "Why don't we all just fucking go home?" (Ven couldn't say a sentence without the word "fuck.")

Then he called me on the two-way radio and said, "The owner left the building."

All the journalists left the scene. And when Ven didn't return to the station with the other reporters, I called him 20 minutes later to ask, "Where are you?"

He was still at the building. And half an hour later, West came out and Ven got an exclusive interview.

Like so many TV personalities, Ven could sometimes be bigger than life—especially on days at the station when we simply didn't have time for lunch. Not so different from other industries, I suppose. But in the news business, we called this taking a lunch penalty. And Ven never took a shine to it.

On those days, without fail, he called me and asked, "When do I get lunch?"

"We're gonna have to take a lunch penalty," I said, bracing for his response.

He barely paused before saying, "If I fuckin' don't get lunch, I'm going to be violating the code."

After the first time we went through this, I knew the "code." But I always played along, asking, "What code?"

"What mother fuckin' code!?" he asked incredulously. "The code of never getting wet, hungry, or shot at! And you can bet that hungry is the most important one!"

Then he bitched, pissed, and moaned about not getting lunch. But it was what it was. It was no skin off my teeth, and he just had to deal with it.

Although he may not have been as well-known as Bill Bonds, Ven had the same propensity for drinking. I once went to the Press Club with him at 10:00 a.m.

"What do you want to drink?" he asked.

I wasn't exactly in the habit of drinking in the morning, but I said, "I'll have a whiskey sour or Southern Comfort sour."

He rolled his eyes and scoffed. "Girly drinks," he said. Then he proceeded to order me something much stronger.

I'm not sure what it was, but they kept coming. And after three more, I was five sheets to the wind. He, of course, was doing just fine. His liver had adjusted to these countless liquid meals—which may have accounted for some of his angst at not getting lunch on those penalty days.

Unfortunately, his liver eventually surrendered. Ven died of liver disease in the 1980s. But he threw a gloriously memorable going away party for himself when he was dying, which was attended by big-name folks like Chrysler Chairman Lee Iacocca and U.S. Senator Donald Riegle. Ven truly was an incredible reporter, and a good man.

After I moved to Chicago and was working at ABC owned and operated WLS-TV, Ven sometimes visited me while on assignment in Chicago for WXYZ. While spending time together over drinks, he would playfully bemoan how the assignment desk was not nearly as professional after my departure.

CONCERTS, COCAINE, AND CONCEPTION

Three years into working at WXYZ, I was still attending music shows whenever possible. I wanted to attend a Springsteen show in Chicago, so I reached out to the production company. A woman named Jean agreed to get me tickets to see him.

I was supposed to meet my friend there to attend the show, but he couldn't make it. So since I had a spare ticket, I asked Jean if she wanted to go. We hit it off and started hanging out. The first time she flew to Detroit to see me, I picked her up and drove her to where I was living—with an old girlfriend who didn't mind. After that, Jean and I flew back and forth on weekends to see each other. She worked for a concert promoter, so we were regulars at concerts, and we had a great time together.

This was 1980, when alcohol and cocaine were big on the scene. No stranger to alcohol, I had tried cocaine once before, but it hurt my nose. Now, however, I experienced it again, and loved everything about it. I was officially hooked.

Cocaine was like candy, and it was everywhere. It seemed that everyone was doing it. In fact, I once attended an after-party for a tennis event where even the biggest tennis stars of that time were doing it—between 2:00 and 4:00 a.m. on a morning before their competition. How would they perform on the courts the next day? As if they'd gotten a solid eight hours' worth of sleep.

As for me, I loved how my new cocaine habit made me feel omnipotent, happy, and upbeat. Although I was already what everyone considered a high-energy person, cocaine amped it up even more. It energized me like I'd never felt before.

In a matter of months, anytime and anywhere was a good place to do it. After all, I never arrived late for work, let alone missed a day. Even on nights when cocaine kept me awake with my heart pounding and racing at 100 miles per minute, I just accepted this as the norm.

When Jean became pregnant with my oldest son, Jason, we eventually married. Becoming a father did not inspire me to stop using cocaine. It just didn't seem like an option. I didn't realize that the cocaine was helping me mask the pain of my childhood. I just knew that it felt incredible, and I didn't feel bad. I craved it.

We discussed whether she'd move to Detroit, or I'd come to Chicago. Since Detroit was in rough shape at that time, and I could more easily land a job in Chicago, we decided on the Windy City. So I bid farewell to WXYZ—the home of my first job in broadcasting.

Shortly before I left for Chicago, Dave Diles—who was then the WXYZ sports director—and reporter Jim Herrington threw me a going away party at the clubhouse where Jim lived.

Just before the party, I went to Dave and told him, "It's been incredible. You've been such a great mentor and even gave me relationship advice—even though you've been married multiple times. Why were you always there for me?"

To my surprise, he grabbed me by my shirt and shoved me up against the wall. "What the fuck is the difference why I did it?" he snarled. "I did it, didn't I? And you better fuckin' do it, too."

I was a little shaken. But I never forgot the gesture—or the lesson. So any time a kid or adult wants direction, guidance or 10 minutes of my time, I remember this. I can honestly say that any time someone has asked to meet with me over the years, I've always said yes, even on days when maybe I felt like saying no.

"Morty" at a suburban Detroit amusement park with pony rides.

"Morty," age 4, with Rocky the parakeet. Unfortunately, days after this picture was taken, Morty's dad, Morris, accidentally stepped on Rocky and Rocky was no more.

Edgar Guest School in Detroit 1958. That's "Morty," top row second from the right. This is the school where the race riot took place the very next year as some parents protested the busing in of Black students whose school burned down.

"Morty" dressed as Wyatt Earp with his grandmother's nurse, Marie DeRose, just prior to his 5th birthday party.

Waldo E. Lessenger School in Oak Park, MI., 1965. Sixth grade graduation composite. That's "Morty," second row from the bottom, far right.

Mort's parents, Morris and Ella Meisner, outside their Oak Park, Michigan home. They paid $6,000 for the house in 1963, had a $38 mortgage payment, yet still were evicted just in time for Thanksgiving the same year, shortly after JFK was assassinated.

"Morty's" bar mitzvah lunch, 1966, with brother, Tony, his wife, Marian and cousin, Pat Small.

Mort 1971 – Oak Park High School graduation photo.

Cousin Alfred Deutsch, with Great Uncle Adolph Deutsch (seated) who put Mort through college and to whom he is forever grateful.

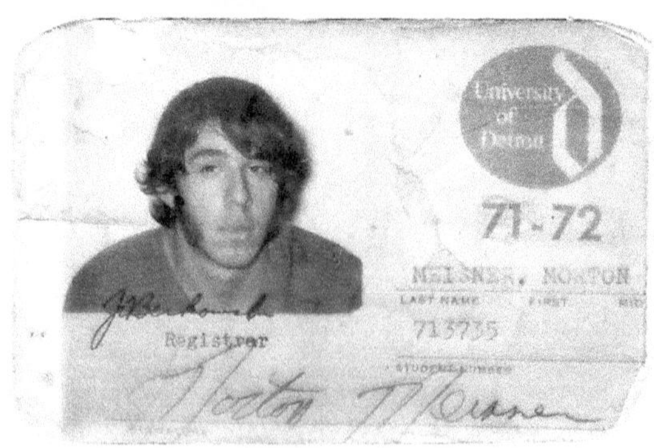

University of Detroit freshman photo ID, 1971. This lovely photo speaks for itself.

Mort visiting with college friend and NBA player, Detroit Piston, Terry Tyler. That's lifelong friend Steve Azoury in the background.

My 1967 Camaro, Lem, in 1973. On my way to visit a girlfriend. The horn on the car never worked except once when someone ran a red light. "I pressed down on the horn instinctively and it worked; the car swerved to miss us." The horn never worked before or after. Divine intervention?

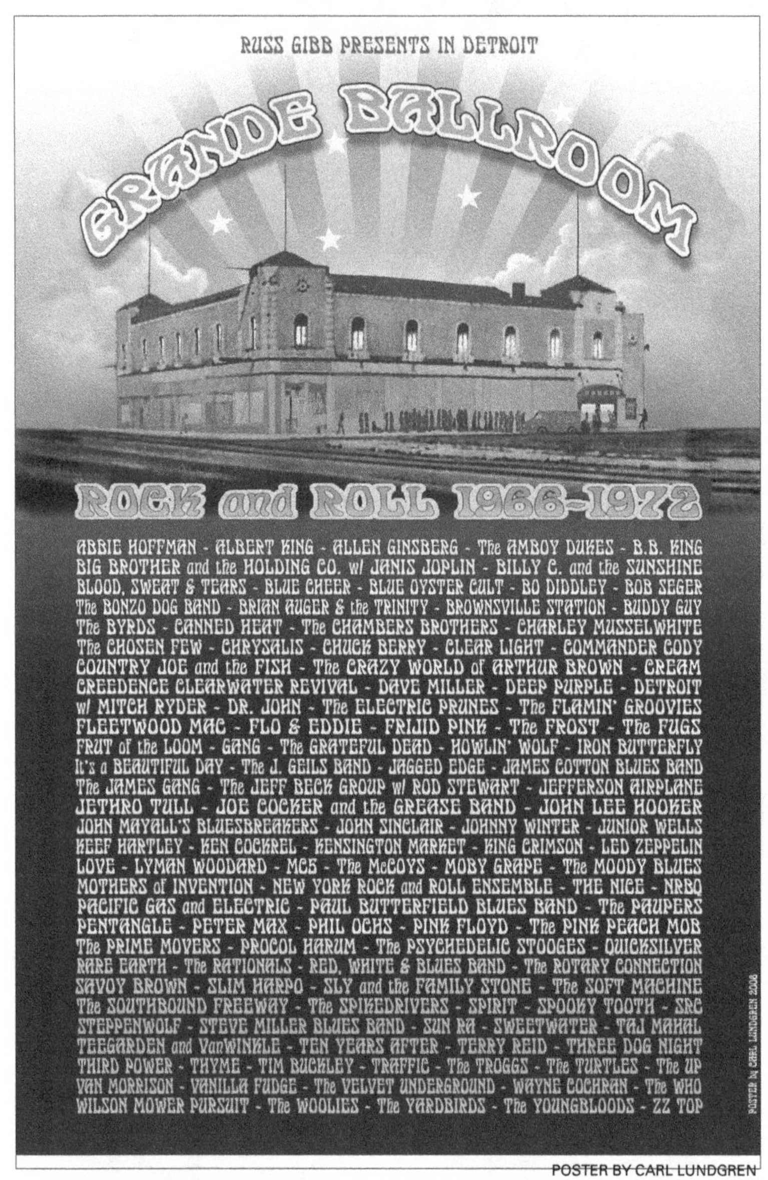

POSTER BY CARL LUNDGREN

Grande Ballroom, Detroit's legendary version of the Fillmore, where everyone who was anyone performed.

POSTER BY CARL LUNDGREN

Poster depicting many of the groups Mort promoted who appeared at a major Detroit arena.

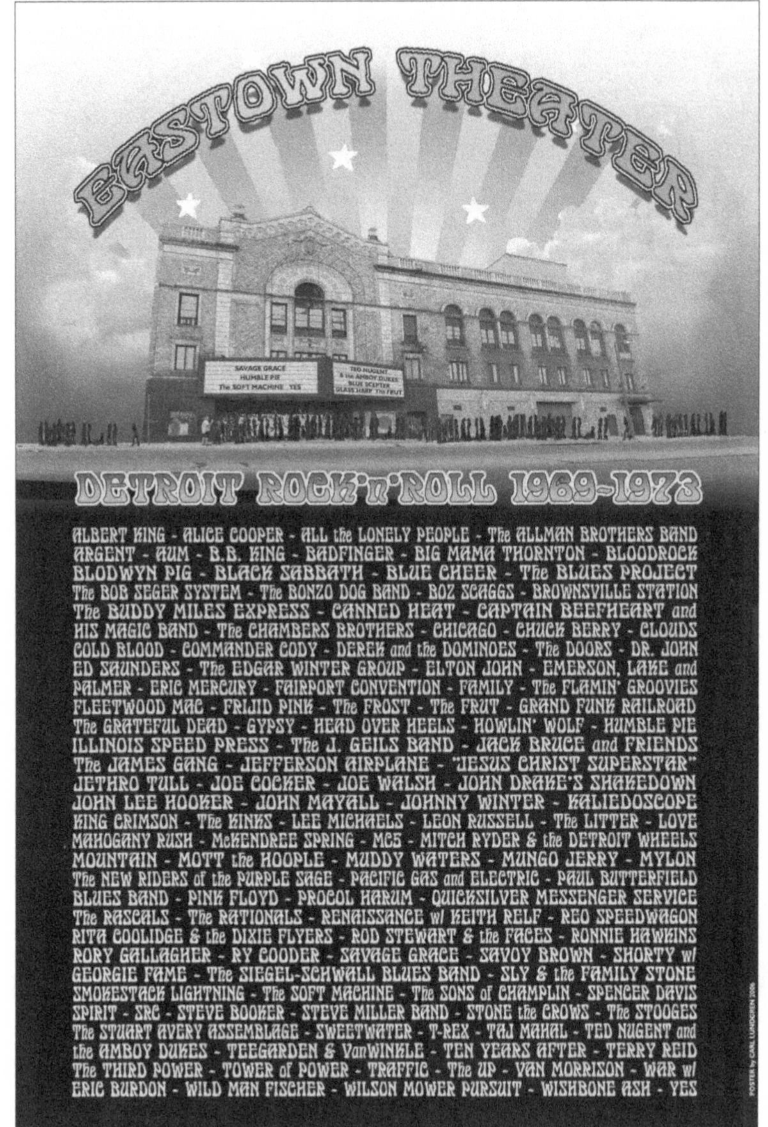

POSTER BY CARL LUNDGREN

Rock royalty like Emerson Lake and Palmer, Elton John, Seger, Cocker, Alice, and Traffic to name a few, were virtual regulars.

POSTER BY CARL LUNDGREN

The Michigan Palace in Detroit where Mort promoted such stars as Bruce Springsteen, Electric Light Orchestra, Bachman-Turner Overdrive, and The MC5.

Mort and friend, the late Nelson Burg, visiting Bruce Springsteen haunt, The Stone Pony in Asbury Park, NJ. This was minutes after leaving the home of Clarence "Big Man" Clemons in Seabright, NJ.

Mort's press pass in 1980 when he worked at ABC O&O WXYZ in Detroit.

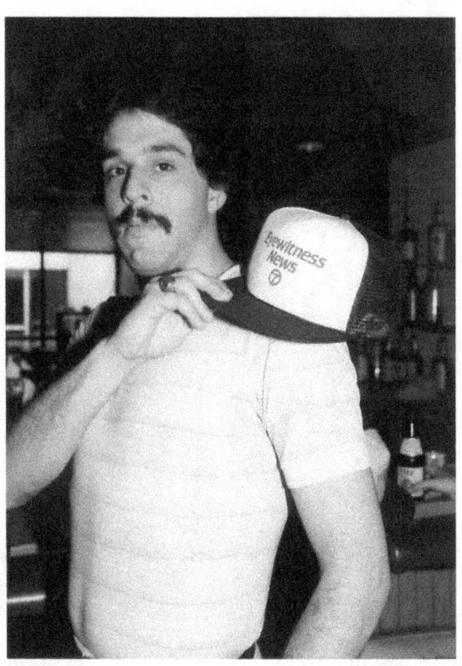

Mort, while at ABC O&O, WLS in Chicago, 1983.

Mort field producing for CBS in Chicago, President Ronald Reagan's visit, September 2nd, 1981. That's CBS reporter Frank Currier with a cigarette dangling out of his mouth over Mort's left shoulder.

Mort, with his parents while at ABC O&O, WLS in Chicago, 1983.

Mort with first born son, Jason, Chicago, 1983.

John Glenn

May 4, 1983

Mr. Nort Meisner
c/o WLS TV
190 N. State
Chicago, Illinois 60601

Dear Nort,

Just wanted to let you know how much Annie and I enjoyed meeting you during our recent trip to Chicago.

The trip is one that we will remember for many years to come. Thank you for your part in making it such a memorable occasion.

We look forward to seeing you again as the campaign continues.

Best regards.

Sincerely,

JOHN GLENN
United States Senator

Post Office Box 1984, Ben Franklin Station Washington, D.C. 20044 (202) 783-1984
Paid for by the John Glenn Presidential Committee.
Robert A. Farmer, Treasurer.

After spending an hour with Senator John Glenn and wife Annie, the forever classy astronaut, American Bad Ass, turned politician, turned presidential candidate, fired off this letter.

John "Bulldog" Drummond, CBS News, WBBM Chicago, bar none, the greatest crime, mob and mafia reporter I have ever worked with.

EMMY: OUTSTANDING TELEVISION NEWSCAST 1986
Mort Meisner, Assignment Manager, KSDK-TV, St. Louis

Mort with the late singing superstar, Lou Rawls, and John Carney, a St. Louis media personality, St. Louis, 1985.

Mort as News Director at Fox O&O WJBK in Detroit, 1988

Press Pass 1991. Mort took pride in being able to roll up his sleeves and investigate/ produce meaningful stories even while serving as News Director, WJBK, Detroit. If you are wondering what WJBK stood for, the call letters at one time stood for Jesus Be Kind.

March 5, 1992

Dear Mort,

Your the best! Now I have a mug for my tea at work and at home!

Thank you so much it is really great!

Best,

Connie

(I noticed I have to careful with how hot the tea is?!)

Connie Chung
CBS News

Mort developed a long-distance friendship with CBS Anchor/Reporter Connie Chung.

DAN RATHER

Dear Mort,

Thank you.

Especially coming from an experienced master pro such as you that letter is deeply appreciated.

Come to see me!

Yours truly,

Dan

26 May 1993

Relationships and friendships with legends like CBS News Anchor and 60 Minutes contributor, Dan Rather, were very meaningful.

Press Pass while News Director at WJBK, FOX O&O in Detroit.

SPORTS FINAL

NEW CROWN HEIGHTS GRAND JURY

EXCLUSIVE

SEE PAGE 5

DAILY NEWS

NEW YORK'S HOMETOWN NEWSPAPER

Friday, January 7, 1994

Pain etches the face of top American figure skater Nancy Kerrigan after she was clubbed at practice yesterday in Detroit.

'WHY ME?'

Maniac attacks Olympic skater

SEE PAGE 3

EMMY – BREAKING STORY 1995 – Kerrigan Attack
Mort Meisner
NEWS DIRECTOR WJBK–TV

Mort as News Director at WJBK in Detroit with (left to right) Assistant News Director, Carla Gaines; Anchor Sherry Margolis; Investigative Reporter, Vince Wade; and Business Anchor and Finance Reporter, Murray Feldman.

Mort with Anchor Rich Fisher at station event featuring Hall & Oates and Carly Simon while at WJBK. Sadly, Fisher has since passed away.

Mort with Glen Campbell at Freedom Hill Amphitheater in suburban Detroit.

A voracious softball player! WJBK, FOX in Detroit sponsored local legendary team. That's Mort top row, 6th from the left with oldest and dear friend Larry Foote to his left. Daughter, Nicole also in top row and son, Mark in bottom row.

Diane Sawyer, ABC News.

Mort built a long distance relationship with one of his heroes, Jackie Gleason. Dad, Morris, was a real-life Ralph Kramden, but drove a cab.

Mort along with current Anchor and client Glenda Lewis and her mother, Anchor Diana Lewis. Glenda is primary female Anchor at ABC affiliate WXYZ in Detroit. Diana set the tone for greatness and Glenda continues to make her own footsteps.

Bill Bonds and Diana Lewis who you will find in the "best of" section of this book. Bonds is the greatest Anchorman Mort ever worked with, or for that matter who anyone ever worked with. Diana is the best and most popular female Anchor to ever work in Detroit. The three of us worked together at ABC O&O WXYZ in Detroit.

Mort with best friend Jim Epperson whom he met in 1985 while at NBC affiliate KSDK in St. Louis. Epperson is a retired top-level executive with AT&T, and a fellow Bruce Springsteen and Southside Johnny fan.

Mort with daughter Nicole and Reverend Jesse Jackson at Berry Gordy's 75th birthday celebration. Mort became friends with Jackson while at CBS and ABC News in Chicago.

Mort coaching son, Mark, while managing the Huntington Woods Cats. Mark went on to play Division 1 Baseball, and is now a Major League Baseball Agent.

Mort with his family, 2018. (left to right) Son-in-law, Neil Brooks; daughter, Nicole Meisner; son, Mark; wife, Leslie; Grandson, Tony; Mort; son, Jason; and his bride, Nan.

OFF TO THE WINDY CITY

My boss in Detroit arranged for me to meet Tom Kuelbs, the news director at WLS in Chicago. The problem was that Tom didn't like my boss. So, even though they flew me in and arranged the meeting, I sat there waiting for quite a while, and people kept walking past me. It seemed that they were freezing me out because of my connection to my former boss back in Detroit.

So I walked over to the local CBS affiliate—unannounced.

"Can I see the news director, Eric Ober?" I asked.

I got in and met with their assignment manager.

"ABC flew me in," I said, "but they refused to meet with me. Do you have a job for me?"

"Nothing at the moment," they said, "but come back in a few hours."

So I did. WBBM-TV hired me as assignment manager/managing editor, which paid as well as what I was making in Detroit. And I needed the money, since I now had a child in the picture.

When I told Phil that I got frozen out, he was pretty upset at WLS management, but reminded me that the door can always swing open again.

During my first hour on the job, I went into the bathroom, where a very short man was taking a leak beside me. It turned out to be the legendary news anchor, Walter Jacobson. He looked at me and said,

"I don't know who the fuck you are, or where the hell you came from, but I wanna tell you, if it doesn't happen in city hall, it isn't news. You come from that happy talk station WXYZ. And you're just a two-bit punk from Detroit."

I could have taken this as a bad sign. But I later learned that the guy had apparently told a friend that they would likely be offered the job, and receive it.

Also during my first day at WBBM, Gene Siskel—already part of the legendary film critic duo Siskel and Ebert—approached my desk.

He flipped a couple of $20 bills at me and said, "Hey, kid. Can you run to Farmer Brown's and get me a couple of slabs of ribs and some hot links?"

I turned to look at him and asked him, half seriously, "Do you know who the fuck I am?"

He said he didn't.

"I'm your fucking new boss," I said.

Then he reached into his pocket, flipped out another $20 and said, "Get yourself a slab, too."

NEWSROOM ANTICS

I saw a lot of things at WBBM. When I think of this era, I often remember one legendary writer and producer who became something of a mentor to me. Smart and talented, he would sit quietly typing news stories at his desk. He mostly kept to himself. This wasn't always easy, given the communal nature of newsrooms.

In fact, it wasn't at all uncommon for everyone to partake in one another's food and drinks in the newsroom. So, one day during a major breaking news story while I was walking around the newsroom and exhorting the troops, he got up to take a leak. As he walked away from his desk, I picked up his cup to take a sip of water. It took me by surprise when I suddenly had a mouthful of whiskey. Neat. No ice. Not watered down. I learned my lesson that day about not sampling and sipping other peoples' drinks. Well, at least not anything this writer/producer had on his desk.

It could have been worse, though. Much worse. As was the case for loved and hated anchorman Walter Jacobson, who received brownies from an adoring fan. As it turned out, the fan either practiced tough love, or was not a fan at all. The brownies were laced with a laxative—Ex-Lax—and, needless to say, Jacobson had an interesting rest of the day. I certainly didn't cry any tears for this man who verbally attacked me in the bathroom just minutes into my new job at WBBM.

As I settled into my position, I was loving Chicago. It felt like a really good fit for me. At the time of my arrival, I spent a good amount of time on the South Side. One of my regular haunts was the Checkerboard, or the C Board as it was known. It was a remarkable Blues Spot where people like Buddy Guy, Lefty Diz, and legends like Junior Wells played. It had everything you'd expect from an old school Chicago blues bar—dark and smokey with a B-movie vibe that was sometimes unsettling. Buddy and a guy named L.C. Thurman owned this South Side mainstay where Mick Jagger and others would sometimes visit and jam.

My first visit to the C Board was especially memorable. I went with a fellow worker named Jim Lucas, who was something of a blues aficionado. He was also a connoisseur of ribs. At any rate, we sat down and took in the scenery—mostly men playing cards, chess, checkers, whatever, smoking cigarettes, cigars, and pipes, and sucking down red beans and rice. A stocky waitress stuffed into a black dress two sizes too small came to our table. Her name was Oretta.

Relatively disinterested, she asked me, "What'll you have?"

"What kind of beer do you have?" I asked.

Oretta cocked her head to the side and raised her eyebrows. "I have green bottles," she paused, "and I have brown bottles."

I foolishly asked again what kind they were.

With a flash of frustration, Oretta struck back with her hands on her hips and said loudly, "I HAVE GREEN BOTTLES AND I HAVE BROWN BOTTLES."

I went for brown.

At some point in the evening, we wound up in the backroom hanging out with the house band, The Rib Tips. They were waiting for someone to come out and front them. They had no drummer. So Buddy asked if anyone could play. Despite having very little experience with the drums, I volunteered. The next thing I knew, there I was, sort of front and center. I wasn't very good, but nobody cared.

I went to the C Board many times over the years. Some nights, I almost had to fight my way out. But on that first night there in 1981, it was magic.

Frank Currier was a crusty curmudgeon whom I loved. I didn't have long to get to know him, though. When I arrived at WBBM, he was preparing to leave to work for CBS News at the network level. Handsome, great news guy who always brought home the bacon, Frank truly had a golden voice and, when motivated, was as good as anyone you could imagine.

Frank's going away party in the newsroom was memorable. Reporters, anchors, and management all toasted Frank. Then it came time for Irv Kupcinet to deliver his toast. Irv, more affectionately known as Kup, was an entertainment and society writer for the *Chicago Sun Times* who did segments for us in the news. He talked like he had a mouth full of marbles. And he was also notoriously absent-minded. So as Kup stood up, Frank took cover under a desk as a joke because he knew at some point the toast would head south.

But Kup took center stage in the newsroom, talking about Frank's accomplishments. It seemed like a perfectly nice toast until he ended it with, "Well, Bob, it's been nice working with you and we all wish you well at CBS."

You just never knew what Kup would say next.

Another great journalist at WBBM was John Quinones, who has become a star reporter and program host at ABC News. Back when we worked together, John was a handsome young guy at a time when TV news had very little Latino on-air presence. On one occasion, I assigned John to cover a murder and the suspect's name was, unfortunately, "Quinones Quinones." We laughed about it, but it was also sadly ironic.

Still, John was, and is, a star in his own right. He has worked in many roles for ABC News over the years, including the *Evening News*, ABC *Prime Time,* and *20/20.* He also hosted his own show called *What Would You Do?* which still airs. Living in the same neighborhood, John (whom I called Johnny Q) and I hung out quite a bit. Once while walking home from a watering hole at 3:00 a.m., we saw White Sox announcer Harry Carey holding up a lamppost on Rush Street. He was coming off a night of serious reverie. John and I looked at each other as if to say, *What the hell is this drunk doing out so late?* But we quickly realized the hypocrisy.

My time at WBBM was during Ronald Reagan's administration. Riding on the wave of being a successful B-actor and ex-governor, Reagan thrived in the public eye. His Star Wars Defense Program was catching steam and all of a sudden, this President whom I'd pretty much regarded as a "let them eat cake" sort of guy was enjoying amazing popularity. Working at a CBS News owned and operated station, we certainly owned the market for any local coverage of Reagan's visits. In fact, under the stellar direction of News Director Eric Ober, we were considered the Cadillac of local news, anywhere in the country.

On the night of September 27th in 1981, I was closing in on one year as assignment manager/managing editor at WBBM. The station was often in a state of chaos—a state that has always been comfortably familiar for me, given my upbringing. Some of the antics were just part and parcel for the news business. Yet, WBBM was also brimming with the super egos of its talent. (In TV news, on-air reporters and anchors are called "the talent.") After a year, I thought I'd seen it all. I was wrong. Nothing I had ever seen or heard prepared me for what would happen that night.

Our weekday sports anchor was Johnny Morris. A retired receiver for the Chicago Bears, Morris was chiseled and handsome with confidence and gusto. He looked like he could easily stroll back onto the field and jump into the game without a second thought. His wife Jeannie was also a sportscaster at WBBM, as well as the author of the book *Brian Piccolo: A Short Season*. This couple dripped with success.

By contrast, our weekend sports anchor Bruce Roberts was a pudgy guy who, with his terribly loud sports coats, appeared to get fashion advice from used car salesmen. Even so, he was well-known by the NFL and had also done quite a lot of work in the world of golf. So while he may not have garnered the attention for his physical appearance that Morris did, he was a respected sports anchor.

That night, Bruce was preparing for his 10:00 p.m. sports segment in his office just off the newsroom. Although it was a Sunday night, I happened to be there, working on a project. As the 10:00 p.m. hour neared, Bruce did not show up at the anchor desk in the newsroom. We all became alarmed. Someone went to his office, hoping that he'd perhaps just lost track of time, though that was unlikely for Bruce.

Bruce was found lying on the floor in his office. We immediately called an ambulance and after the EMT personnel worked on him a while with little success, he was taken to nearby Northwestern Hospital. To no avail, though. They said it was likely that he'd been pretty much gone from the moment he hit the floor.

This disturbing scenario was made worse by the fact that it was a Sunday night in September, and we needed to deliver NFL football highlights on air. In the spirit of "the show must go on," political reporter Mike Flannery grudgingly stepped in for Bruce. Flannery knew very little about sports and cared even less. As luck would have it, the highlights from that particular Sunday were abundant with crucial kicks for field goals and extra points. This wouldn't have been such a big deal, had this not been the era of foreign-born kickers in the NFL. Suffice it to say, Flannery's attempt to pronounce names like Uwe von Schamann and Fuad Reveiz were epic fails. It was a sad and surreal evening, to say the least.

It didn't come as any surprise that the broadcast figureheads like Walter Jacobson were just as egomaniacal in Chicago as they were in Detroit. One day, Walter's bluster came to a head. And I wasn't going to sit idly by and take it.

The deposed Jimmy Carter frequently came to Chicago to visit his son and grandchildren. He received Presidential treatment and deference in how we covered him. We always sent a crew, just in case something went down. But nothing ever really did. As such, we didn't always do a story on him being in town. During one such visit, Walter walked stridently up to my desk and said, "Are you aware that President Carter was in town today?"

I looked up at him—which, given his short stature, could only be accomplished when I was sitting and he was standing. "Yes, I am," I said.

He cocked his brows. "Then why didn't we cover him?"

"We did," I responded, referring to the fact that we'd sent a crew but that nothing had happened.

"Why didn't we do a full-blown story on him?"

And I just said, "It's not news. There's no point in doing a story about Carter walking his grandchild for the sixth time."

Walter just lost it. He started blowing up and went nose-to-nose with me. He stuck a finger in my face and began yelling at me—all the while inviting attention from everyone else. Even those who affectionately called him Jake.

"Do you like working here?" he finally asked with a threatening tone.

"Not in particular," I said, feeling heated, "because I don't like you."

"Oh yeah!? Well, I'll call Gene Jankowski and make sure you get fired then!" he yelled. Jankowski ran CBS News and was one of the people who could easily get me fired. I didn't care.

"Get the fuck out of my face," I yelled back, waving him away.

He stared into my eyes and tweaked me across the nose!

"You just alienated the most important man in journalism," he said. Then he turned on his heels and walked back to his desk, where his assistants sat behind him like a pack of rats.

I was approaching a rage. And even though I had a broken leg from a tackle football game, I hobbled over to him. To do what? Honestly, I was ready to beat the shit out of him for everything he'd ever done to anyone at all. I got right in his face.

"If you ever touch me again," I growled, "I'll put my foot so far up your ass, it will come out of your mouth."

"And I'll be in back of him applauding," I heard from behind me. I turned and saw the general manager. He'd been warned that a brawl was about to break out and came to settle it. After he made his statement, the whole newsroom broke into applause. Walter was stunned and speechless. But it was so close to the time he had to get ready to do the newscast, he was unable to respond.

My relationship with Walter didn't improve after that. But strangely, it didn't get worse, either. The truth was, despite an ego multiple times the size of his small physical stature, Walter was an outstanding journalist. He was wired in with sources, and broke stories. For that, I respected him.

Walter would increasingly praise me—though grudgingly—as I often delivered exclusive stories.

Bill Kurtis co-anchored with Jacobson. He was far from the blow-hard windbag that Walter was. But he wasn't exactly the deepest guy either.

I used to sit in the newsroom every day about 20 minutes before the news started. It was customary for Bill to stroll through the studio, casually applying ChapStick, then snap his fingers at everybody, saying hello.

One day, I was in a bit of a dour mood. I'd just received some bad news. Bill strolled up to me and asked how I was doing. So I answered him honestly.

"Well, my grandma died and I have to go to Detroit for the funeral," I said.

He smiled, snapped his fingers and responded, "Great! Keep up the good work."

This was not malicious whatsoever. He simply wasn't listening. He never did.

Another guy who was always good for a laugh was Frank Gardner, one of the news directors during my time at WBBM. Although he was small in stature, he had some pretty big expressions. When someone was mad, he referred to them as "hotter than a fresh fucked fox in a pepper patch." Or if someone was stupid, he said they were "a couple bubbles off plumb."

Anyhow, Frank was a nice guy with good people skills and even better news judgment. So, many times when I walked into his office and told him about a story I wanted to cover, he immediately asked, "Who's gonna do it?"

"We don't have a lot of people," I answered, "so I'm going to need to use so and so."

"There may be a good story there," he nodded and paused. "But he ain't gonna get it." And he was always right.

Of course, this was a different era. Managers said things that would not be tolerated today. For example, there was one assignment guy whom I liked. He was young and combative, though, and one manager felt he needed a little dressing down. So he had me bring the assignment guy into his office and just stated succinctly, "I oughta kick your white WASP-y ass around the block until it turns red."

LIVING DOWN A BLUNDER OVER COMEDIAN'S DEATH

The day that 33-year-old actor/comedian John Belushi was found dead from an apparent drug overdose in Hollywood had been just another day in the WBBM newsroom. Up until the moment I received that news, that is.

This was a big story. The fact that Belushi was a Chicago native made it even bigger. Naturally, our newsroom swung into action in an attempt to get reactions from those who knew him. Gene Siskel, who worked for us, was tapped. John's brother Jim Belushi was contacted, too. It was my tough and self-assigned job to reach out to his mother, Agnes Belushi. I spent 15 to 20 minutes trying to find her phone number from various sources, but kept coming up empty-handed. I finally managed to get it from a private investigator.

I nervously dialed her home phone number. It was mid-afternoon in early March and I'd felt just a hint of spring in the air while outdoors earlier that day. It was a combination of newness and promise. Yet here I was, preparing to interview a mother who was dealing with the fact that her son was gone.

After several rings, she answered.

"Is this Agnes Belushi?" I asked.

"Yes," she said, with slight apprehension. "This is Agnes."

"Agnes, this is Mort Meisner from WBBM and I'm so terribly sorry for the loss of your son, John."

At that moment, I realized that I'd imagined the apprehension in her voice. After a prolonged, dead silence, I realized that she hadn't yet heard the news and that I'd just told her that her son was dead. My throat tightened and my stomach felt like it dropped ten feet. I was absolutely sickened.

While I had made similar calls dozens of times, I'd never had this particular experience. When I realized what had just gone down, I apologized and let her go. It was a tough moment that stays with me still today.

NEWSROOM PERSONALITIES TO REMEMBER

One of my favorite reporters was John "Bulldog" Drummond. John was a crime reporter who probably looked like a gum shoe when he was born. He wore old 1940s suits with his pockets filled with news clips about the mafia. He also liked covering stories about Nazi war criminals, the mafia, and low-level thugs in general.

In fact, we covered the trial of Conrad Schellong—one of the first Nazi war criminals brought to trial in the 1980s. As Schellong made his way into the courthouse hallway, John pushed his way to the front so he could interact with him. He clicked his heels and said, "Heil, Hitler."

When Schellong did it in return, John just sneered at him and said, "You Nazi son of a bitch."

John didn't know the meaning of fear. He had dealings with some horrifying mobsters, too. Among them: James "Legs" D'Antonio, a driver for the mafia. That's a bigger deal than it may sound. You can imagine the kind of things he saw. Then there was Joey "the Clown" Lombardo, who was known for hanging people alive on meat hooks. John also had connections with Joseph Doves Aiuppa and Anthony "the Big Tuna" Accardo—mob guys. He covered them all. And whenever he left for vacation, he left me a white paper telling me where to find what clip or video—just in case a mobster was "liquidated" while he was out of town.

One of John's less endearing qualities was thriftiness. This is a kind way of saying that he was cheap. And if you ever went out with him, you were guaranteed to foot the bill. His classic move was to wait until the bill came, say he had to go take a leak, then leave the establishment and stand outside, waiting.

But considering everything I learned from John, paying the tab seemed like more than a fair tradeoff.

John was one of the most eccentric reporters I knew. But he certainly didn't have the market cornered. Harry Porterfield was equally in the running for that moniker.

News Anchor Harry Porterfield spoke of himself in the third person. Truly. And he'd started a twice-weekly series of reports called "Someone You Should Know." The main problem was, nine out of ten stories involved people missing an arm, a leg, or all four. He did a story one day on a parking lot attendant who had no legs and stood on crutches all day to wave people in and out. For some reason in Harry's mind, the qualifier for "someone you should know" had to be missing a limb. Anyhow, Frank Gardner told me to tell him to stop doing the stories and find people who were ambulatory.

Another problem with Harry was that he only liked to work from 11:00 a.m. until 7:00 p.m.

"You need to come in at nine," I told him.

He looked at me and said, "Harry Porterfield doesn't come in at nine."

And I told him, "Then Harry Porterfield doesn't have a job if he doesn't come in at nine."

One of the most unsavory characters at WBBM was legendary newsman Dick Goldberg. I met him when he was an executive producer at WBBM. A bully through and through, Goldberg was arrogant, tough, and sarcastic, but very smart. He tried to intimidate me, and when I broke stories, he attempted to stop them from airing. It was all out of spite. No surprise, he and Jacobson were bosom buddies. Birds of a feather.

The thing with bullies, though, is that most of them eventually get their comeuppance. For Goldberg, it happened two years later at WLS when my boss at that time, Bill Applegate, hired Goldberg. The night that Harold Washington, Chicago's first Black mayor, was about to win the office, I had arranged for my station and anchor/reporter Jack Jones to be with Washington exclusively when the polls closed to get his reaction to what would someday be considered an historical event.

In a hotly contested race, Washington had managed to beat Bernard Epton, a white Jewish Republican who'd run a dirty and disgusting campaign that painted Washington as a liar, a crook, and even a child molester. It was ludicrous, to say the least. Washington was a friend and a good man who would end up being a great mayor.

In any case, Goldberg told me he was not interested in the exclusive I'd arranged. Insanity, I thought. So I went to inform Applegate of Goldberg's decision and he told me to get Goldberg into his office. I was only too happy to oblige. Applegate lit into Goldberg and pounded his finger on his chest—ordering him to air the interview I had arranged.

So began the beginning of the end for Goldberg at WLS. He had been neutered and was meek as a lamb moving forward. He even tried to be friendly to me and would try to kiss my ass. I, of course, would have none of it.

LOVING CHICAGO AS A GREAT NEWS TOWN

Getting married, having my first son, and moving to Chicago definitely afforded news opportunities that never would have happened back in Detroit at that time.

For example, when Mother Teresa visited the United States in 1983, Detroit was not on the itinerary. Understandably. Detroit was struggling hard at that time. (Apparently, even Mother Teresa had her limits.) But Chicago was thriving. And Mother Teresa had a scheduled stop there.

Mother Teresa based her life's work on helping the downtrodden. So, she was scheduled to visit the ghetto of Chicago on the morning we were to interview her. It didn't matter to me. I was thrilled that I was going to have the chance to do the interview.

The anchorwoman did not feel the same, though. Especially given the time of the interview.

"Wait? You want me to come in at five in the morning to interview a fucking nun?" she asked.

"It's *Mother Teresa*," I said.

"Mother Fucking, I don't care," she said disrespectfully.

It was all in the name of griping, though. The anchorwoman did come in early to interview Mother Teresa, and despite her ignorance of her subject, the result was a great story.

Meanwhile, my many Detroit connections proved helpful while covering certain stories in Chicago. For example, when Jane Byrne was the mayor of Chicago, she appointed school Superintendent Dr. Ruth Love.

But Love didn't have much love for Byrne. So she had her office bugged, then proceeded to blame Byrne for doing it. Unfortunately for her, the guy she had bug it was her Deputy Superintendent Charles Mitchell, whom I already knew from Detroit because he'd been a school official in Highland Park, a Detroit suburb. And because of this connection, we were able to break the story, which led to the demise of Dr. Ruth Love's tenure in Chicago.

SEX, DRUGS & JOURNALISM

It's no big secret now that back then, Chicago newsrooms were incestuous and drug-infested. People were carrying on in a sexually and drug-charged atmosphere both within newsrooms and between newsrooms at other stations. Sometimes, people were having sex in one office while others were doing drugs in other offices. It was pervasive. I was there. I saw it first hand, at least on the drugs side.

One night, a number of us managers were using cocaine at a bar. This wasn't unusual. We would, of course, go into the bathroom to use it, and we followed a protocol. The last one in would leave the package under the toilet seat. On this particular night when it was my turn, I went in and tried to pick it up. The snow seal, as it was called, broke, and $500.00 worth of product literally went down the drain. Oh, well. So be it.

It may still surprise a lot of people that these drug and sex extravaganzas weren't restricted to the behind-the-scenes people or senior managers who had a lot to lose. Many came from the talent ranks. Sometimes we all attended large gatherings and meetings in hotel boardrooms featuring long lines of cocaine, bottles of expensive champagne, and well-known, big-named figures I won't bother to mention here. It really was a lurid scene.

But that's just how it was back then. And it's a time that I'm grateful to regard only in the rearview mirror these days.

During my time in Chicago, one of my goals was to meet Mike Royko, the late Pulitzer Prize-winning columnist for the city's papers.

I considered him the greatest columnist in the world. In fact, I still do.

He was a gun control advocate and wrote a lot about stupid things people did with guns—such as shooting off body parts, killing loved ones, et cetera. Six months into Chicago, I was at a local watering hole with my friend Jim Lucas, who knew the city inside and out. I said to him, "There's Royko!"

Jim warned me not to approach him, but nothing was going to stop me. I went up to Royko.

"Hi Mike, I'm Mort Meisner," I said. "Assignment manager at WBBM. I think you're the greatest columnist ever, anywhere."

With a drink in his right hand, he looked directly at me. He made a circular motion with his left hand and said clearly and succinctly, "Who gives a fuck what you think."

I didn't know whether to laugh or cry. I think I did a little of both. But even though he was trying to embarrass me, he had no idea how immune I was to embarrassment. My father taught me that. Of course, a burgeoning coke habit played into that sense of invincibility, too.

One of the first legitimate scares I experienced around cocaine involved a courier at WBBM. Back then, every good newsroom had couriers. They picked up film, and later, tapes. Sometimes they picked up lunch/dinner for the newsroom. Oftentimes, they shuttled talent to and from the stations.

In Chicago, one well-known courier was a cocaine supplier for *all* the newsrooms. He'd cornered the market. At any rate, since my apartment was on his "route," he offered to drive me home one night. I accepted.

As we were driving, he turned to me and said, "Hey. I've just got one more stop to make tonight. You mind?"

"No, man. Not at all."

So, he pulled up to this questionable nightclub around 7:00 p.m. on a Friday night and we were led into an office occupied by a burly-looking mobster type. The courier pulled out a package of cocaine.

The mobster guy looked at him sideways and mumbled, "This looks short."

"It's not," the courier said.

The man nodded and observed the package. "You better hope it's not," he said. "Because if it is, I'll kill you," he said to the courier. Then he turned to me. "And I'll kill him, too."

Fortunately, it turned out it was not "short" and we were allowed to leave. It was frightening as hell. But not enough to make me quit using. Because cocaine continued to numb pain in a way that nothing else had or could. And it seemed the more cocaine I did, the more I wanted to do. I hadn't taken to doing it early in the morning or during the day, though. It was always an after work thing. I considered the time I wasted waiting for the dealer to stop by a necessity. It felt like the right thing to do because of how it made me feel. If I started to feel guilty about it, I'd simply chase it away with a Sea Breeze while I waited for that evening's delivery.

Plus, when I had cocaine, I was never alone. People knew I had it, so they always wanted to hang out. As my usage continued, I occasionally woke up exhausted and thought, *no more.* Later in the day though, I'd use again. The highs crashed into sleepless nights, as the drug made my heart pound fast and hard.

After one such night, I bounced out of bed at 5:00 a.m., hit the shower, got dressed, and told myself, "You feel fine." I hit my hair up with some hair spray, only to find out it was actually a "scrubbing bubbles" kind of product. I stared at myself in the mirror—a foaming, proliferating mess in the hair on my head. I simply wiped it out and went to work. Nothing was going to stop me from using cocaine. After all, it was plentiful. And it was a lifestyle for my friends and colleagues.

Late one night—after my lifestyle had cost me my marriage and home life with my son—my friend Carol was over and we were enjoying a typical cocaine weeknight.

She looked at me thoughtfully and said, "Cocaine is robbing you of your boyish good looks."

I was only 30 years old. It was upsetting—but only for a moment. I considered what she said, then started back up, minutes later. After she left, I felt noticeably more depressed. I thought maybe it was time to quit. These thoughts carried into the next day, as guilt and shame seeped in while I considered where I was with this growing problem. So, what did I do? I bought more. After all, it was precisely what I needed to numb the guilt, shame, and hatred of who I was and who I was becoming.

My behavior became riskier.

I'll never forget the night I was in Lincoln Park in the car with a friend and two women. We had alcohol and cocaine. A cop rapped on the window at 2:00 a.m.

"You're violating curfew," he said. "I could arrest you and impound the car." Then a crooked smile spread across his face. "For $250, we can make this go away."

I played it cool. By this time, I was working at WLS and I flashed him my business card. Then I simply said, "Do you think *this* could make it go away?"

Knowing that what he did was illegal and feeling completely defeated, the cop told us to fuck off and walked away. We were saved from the classic Chicago cop shake down. And I felt an unbridled power begin to take me over. But like all illusions, it would soon fade.

NAVIGATING NEWSROOM POLITICS

I was at WLS when I received a credible FBI tip that Jimmy Hoffa was the subject of a dig near Philadelphia. Since I was in Chicago, I went to my boss to tell him about the tip.

He looked at me in a way that conveyed he had no idea why I was just standing there telling him about it.

"So, grab a reporter, charter a goddamned plane, and go!" he said. That's exactly what I did. After several days there, it was clear that there was no body. Hoffa or otherwise.

Anyhow, the invoice for the plane and other travel showed up several months later. I was ordered to immediately go to the office of our general manager, who is a legendary heavyweight to this day in the industry.

As I entered his office, our general manager held the invoice in his hand and began shaking it in the air. "Who authorized this!?" he asked.

I told him that my boss, who was sitting right there in the office, had ordered it.

He gave me his patented icy stare and said, "Like hell I did!"

When all was said and done, the invoice got paid. But that event would be the beginning of the end for me at WLS.

Every job environment has its own challenging politics. The politics at WLS, however, often went beyond challenging. They could be downright volatile and vengeful.

For example, at WLS I worked with the worst person—and possibly worst reporter—I ever met in the industry. When assigned stories, this reporter would miss the mark nine out 10 times. Completely. It was clear she needed to be fired. What made it tricky was that she was a Black female and she was constantly raging on that the only reason she was getting criticism was because of this fact.

In reality, she was just terrible at her job. So in the spirit of sensitivity, it was decided the best thing to do was put her on probation. It was also decided that I would be the one to tell her.

So, my boss pulled this reporter and me into his office and told me to break the news to her. It didn't go well.

The woman went silent, took a deep breath, then completely unleashed. "You think you can put me on probation!? Fuck you, motherfucker!" she said, absolutely indignant. "I'm tired of all you white motherfuckers fucking me with your big white dicks!"

At which point my boss smiled at her charming words and said, "Well, that's going to make things much easier then." She was eventually let go.

Meanwhile, another woman who worked for me was very smart, talented, and resourceful. Unfortunately, she had it in for one of my producers, who was a prissy and often mean-spirited and spiteful character. So, she decided one day to drop a dime on the DEA and tell them that this producer was dealing drugs out of her Gold Coast Apartment. The DEA promptly responded by ransacking and tearing apart her place. They, of course, found nothing because this woman would not know cocaine powder from talcum powder. It was simply meanness perpetrated against her.

Unfortunately, the situation led to the hastening of my being fired. Although I had nothing to do with it, my name was linked with the dropping of the dime.

On a Black Friday in 1984, a bunch of us were fired from WLS. One reason was suspicion that we were doing coke (which we were). But the reality is, almost everybody was. So, it was more than just that.

We had new bosses at that time—one of whom runs FOX News now. They ran a pretty tight ship and were not, let's just say, particularly fond of us. We were soon gone.

Hours after I was let go, Dick Reingold, who ran NBC's WMAQ in Chicago, called and asked me to meet him at the Ambassador Hotel later that day to discuss working for him.

He offered me an assignment manager job on the spot.

"Can I think about it overnight?" I asked.

"No," he said. "If the shoe doesn't fit, then you shouldn't wear it.

The deal is off the table."

This was the first time since I was 15 that I didn't have a job. And though I made some attempts to find work, I'd taken mostly to hanging out on the beach and smoking weed, which was cheaper than coke. But that doesn't mean I stopped using coke. I just found new ways to get my fix.

THE NINE-MONTH GESTATION PERIOD

It would be nine months between getting fired at WLS and landing my next job. During that time, I was looking for work. I interviewed often and talked to a lot of people. Some negativity around my firing made it tough to get work. Even though money was running out, I still relied on my cocaine. I was building up cash advances and a lot of debt on my credit card. This might have gotten me through to the next gig, had life not had other plans for me.

On February 14th, 1985, my sister-in-law, Mary McClellan, called to tell me that my father was in the hospital.

"What happened?" I asked.

"I didn't hear from your parents for several days," she said. "So I went over to check on them. I found your father on the kitchen floor, and your mother was going about her business."

Mary then explained that, unbeknownst to either of them, my father had a heart attack four days before that. My mother had begged him to call an ambulance. My father, forever victimized by his pride, said he wouldn't allow it. Instead, he lay there on the kitchen floor, peeing on himself and refusing to go to the hospital while she worked around him. I immediately drove home to Detroit to visit him at the hospital.

My father wasn't doing what they asked of him at the hospital. No big surprise there. But I thought I could cheer him up if I gave him an autographed picture or some other item from Willie Horton, the famed left fielder for the Detroit Tigers. So I called down to Lakeland, Florida to see if I could get anything for him. They said they couldn't help me until after spring training ended and the team returned to Detroit.

That's when I phoned Willie Horton directly at the Lakeland Holiday Inn. He agreed to sign a Detroit Tigers cap and sent it UPS. I gave it to my dad.

"You need to do what the doctors are telling you to do," I told him.

But he continued to be difficult. Even in this weakened stage.

During his time in the hospital, my father seemed smaller somehow. Though he was a big fan of profanity, I rarely heard my father say "fuck." He punched *me* in the mouth once for asking what the word meant when I was eight years old. Now, he said, "I don't want to end up in the fucking ground like a turnip in the middle of February." I implored him to fight harder, but beyond that, it was out of my control.

Ultimately unable to do anything else to help him, I returned to Chicago.

I visited my dad a few more times, hoping he'd improve. Then one night, I was at my brother's house when Leslie, whom I had married in 1984, and I were visiting from Chicago, we got a call from a hospital employee named Julius. He reported that my father wasn't doing well. He was bleeding out. As my brother and I were entering the hospital, we passed a Black man. For some reason, I felt compelled to ask him his name. He said it was Julius. Coincidentally, he was going to the Red Cross to get blood for my dad.

The doctors and nurses did everything they could to try to stabilize him. But nothing was working. The only option was to put a balloon in him. As they rolled him into surgery, I noticed they'd outfitted him with a football helmet. Medical technology wasn't quite what it is today and my dad needed the helmet because they'd attached something to the chin guard to stabilize the tube they were putting down his throat to stop the bleed. The ironic thing was that my father *hated* football. Always had. He often said it was the dumbest sport in the world—though he usually opted for more choice words than "dumb." Seeing that helmet, I figured we were doomed. And we were.

After the surgery, the doctor came to us, his face long and drawn. After telling us about tremendous blood loss, as well as brain damage, the doctor said with absolute certainty, "You don't want this."

He said that my father wouldn't have any sort of quality of life in that state. My brother and I had to make the tough decision to take him off life support. Then they pronounced my father dead. It was 3:17 p.m. on Thursday, March 14, 1985. We all went in and it was surreal. There was my dad, 70-year-old Morris Meisner, this once huge, powerful, and blustery man—now lying there dead. Gone. Funny, but several years earlier, my dad bemoaned the fact that he didn't have a middle name to put on his gravestone when he eventually died. Fortunately for him, the always forward thinking and anticipatory dad of mine pulled out of thin air the name Saul and took it as his middle name, which now appears on his gravestone between Morris and Meisner.

I wondered how my mother would handle the loss. I only had to wait about eight minutes to find out. "I want to go home," she said to me. "I need to see my shows. And I want a milkshake."

I stared at her, dumbfounded. "Mom, your husband of 46 years just fucking died."

"I don't care," she said, "I want to leave."

Arguing with her was pointless. We certainly weren't going to bring my father back to life by staying at the hospital. And honestly, I'm not sure she even wanted that.

"I'll drive you home," I said, "and we'll stop for ice cream on the way." She nodded, gathered her coat and other belongings, and we left. We stopped at Baskin-Robbins near her house.

"Ella!" called out Gordon Rubin, the owner. "Where you been?"

"Eh, my husband's been sick."

"Ah," he said. "Sorry to hear that. So how is Morris?"

"He just died," she said as though he'd asked her about a houseplant. "And I want a double chocolate malt."

All I could do was shake my head. That was just part of the crazy life I led. After we left the store, I dropped my mother off at the house so she could watch her shows.

That night, my brother and I met up with our cousin Alan Small and we went downtown Detroit to toast my dad at Lafayette Coney Island, a legendary restaurant that serves chili dogs 24 hours a day, 365 days a year. Funny thing is, my dad always hated this place. Had he been with us, he would have only had a cup of coffee and a piece of pie.

Lafayette remains a place where kings and peasants have always dined together. On any given night, you can see tuxedoed men and women in gowns sitting at the counter or Formica tables on decades-old stools and chairs. "The Coney" never closes. That is, until the Coronavirus took the nation and our city hostage, forcing its temporary closure.

The days that followed my dad's death were strange, to say the least. I couldn't fully grasp that my father was gone. He'd been such a force in my life. And knowing that I'd never hear his bellowing voice again left me feeling a little unmoored.

The reality that he was gone, though, really struck me when we went to Ira Kaufman Chapel to buy a coffin. With no job and a maxed-out credit card, I was in no position to pay funeral costs. The cheapest coffin was $600. But because my father was so large, they told us that my dad probably wouldn't fit in it very well. They actually tried to "fat shame" us into buying another coffin! We weren't having it, though. We went with the cheapest one and he was stuffed into it like a sausage. I finished the ensemble by placing a Detroit Tigers cap on his head—though not the autographed one. It was appropriate, though. In my father's book, baseball was far superior to football.

After returning to Chicago, I felt renewed and was ready to really get serious about getting back to work. But life had one more detour in store for me. This time, it was in the form of emergency gallbladder surgery. The irony wasn't lost on me. I'd had steady work and health insurance for over a decade. But as soon as I lost that insurance, I needed surgery. While healthcare wasn't as heinous as it is now, Leslie and I weren't in any position to pay out-of-pocket for full-on surgery.

Plus, unbeknownst to Leslie, my credit card bills had gotten out of hand as a result of my continued cocaine use. So, my only option was to file for bankruptcy.

Finding work quickly became the TOP priority.

GOING OFF THE DEEP END IN ST. LOUIS

The dry spell finally broke and I was offered three jobs in St. Louis, Cincinnati, and Los Angeles. I already knew that Los Angeles would be the death of me. Too much boozing and drugging happened there. I'd decided to break from cocaine at that point—some of it out of fear of finding work and then getting fired again.

But mostly, I was happy that I felt okay without it. That seemed like a big step. And I was concerned that being in Los Angeles would reignite my habit. So I turned down that offer. Even if it hadn't driven me to heavy drug use, it was a good decision. The guys who were going to hire me there got fired three months later. Had I gone, I would have been out of that job, too.

So I found myself wavering between Cincinnati and St. Louis.

Pat Minarcin was a legendary broadcast guy in Cincinnati. He was a mini version of Bill Bonds—controversial, outrageous, big voice, and good news guy. He was begging me to come to work for him there. I liked Cincinnati. I still do. It's a great town. But at that time, I knew it had some racial issues. So after my interview, on my way to the airport, I asked the Black driver what it was like living there.

"Would you say there are racial problems here?" I asked.

The man just shook his head and said, "No, there ain't no problems here. Because us Negros know our place." His answer sickened me. And I took it as a sign that Cincinnati was not where I belonged. Of course, St. Louis was far from free of race problems. But the driver's comment felt like an obvious omen.

So, I headed off to St. Louis to work at the struggling KSDK—the NBC affiliate—as managing editor with Steve Antoniotti. I've always regarded Steve as a great man with a hot temper. He once yelled so loud at someone that the glass in his office window shook. Even so, I am privileged to be the godfather for his son, Steven.

Among the plenty of other characters at KSDK was an anchor who was grizzled and in his late 50s or early 60s. He was an all-around good guy, good journalist, and good reader. I could never figure out why he wore such short shorts, though. On his birthday, someone sent him a greeting service. This was a huge mistake. The guy showed up right before the 5:00 p.m. broadcast dressed as Groucho Marx and singing Happy Birthday. The anchor literally picked up the poor guy and threw him out the double doors.

LIFELONG FRIENDSHIP FORGED ON ROUGH ROAD TO RECOVERY

The single best thing about taking that job in St. Louis ultimately had nothing to do with broadcasting.

On the Fourth of July in 1985, my life forever changed for the better. Tripp Frohlichstein (who worked at our rival KMOX) invited me to the rooftop fireworks party of the Southwestern Bell building. I didn't know many people in town, so I was only too happy to go. That's when I met James Epperson. He became my best friend—ever—and still is to this day. Jim and I were inseparable and did everything together. He even gave me a special nickname: Bubba. Our families also became very close.

Several years later, Jim demonstrated just how much he cared as a true friend, after I checked into a treatment center in St. Louis. This was the first time I was seeking help for cocaine addiction, and I was so grateful that Jim visited me and even joined me to attend lectures on substance abuse. On one such occasion, I attempted to chat with him while the speaker was talking about addiction and his personal battles. Jim looked over at me and said: "Hold on Bubba, I think he's talking about me."

So you see, we even have drugs and alcohol in common. As such, we attended Alcoholics Anonymous meetings together. At first, we compared our challenges to others, most times saying, "We aren't all that bad." But we were not unlike others whose recovery leads to a long, bumpy road with many ups and downs. The two of us stuck to it, and celebrated little victories, one day at a time. Since Jim's retirement from corporate America, he works feverishly every day to help people get into recovery—and stay there.

Years later, after I moved back to Detroit and my mother Ella passed away, I was delivering the eulogy for her at a local funeral home. I looked up and saw Jim, profusely perspiring on that hot day in June of 1992. He had flown in from Texas and barely made it to the service.

HITTING ROCK BOTTOM AND LEAVING COCAINE IN THE PAST

On October 18, 1989, I stopped using cocaine forever. At first, fear made me quit. But fear couldn't sustain my abstinence. Eventually, I just got so sick and tired of being sick and tired. And when I drove myself to a Detroit-area hospital one night with my heart pounding, pulse racing—sure I was having a heart attack—I hit my rock bottom.

At the time, my doctor was encouraging me to get long-term help.

"Fuck that, Bubba," Jim said, standing over my hospital bed. "You've gotta get honest, or you're gonna die."

These were probably the most powerful words anyone ever said to me. That day, he flew—unbeknownst to me—from Texas as soon as he heard I was in the hospital.

Jim is still my best friend. We only see each other every few years, but we talk and text several times a week. If I hadn't taken that job in St. Louis, I never would have met him. He's caring, compassionate, smart, and loving—all that one could expect from a best friend. It doesn't hurt that he's also a Bruce Springsteen fanatic.

TALES FROM THE NEWSROOM

Back at work, Steve told me I would be working with another executive producer: Carla Gaines. She was a big personality. The first day we met, she walked in wearing a sheer blouse and bright red lipstick. She was short and stocky, and I couldn't help but notice that a dried piece of pasta was stuck on her blouse. Upon our introduction, she said:

"We'll get along just fine as long as you don't cross me."

This statement was strange—given that I would be her boss. And you can bet we had some troubles and difficulties. Especially at the onset. But in the end, I respected her and enjoyed working with her. She was smart and placed a premium on doing a good job. And for as much of a pain in the ass as she could be, I was no walk in the park either. In fact, Carla and I became inseparable—even when we were both being insufferable. Or perhaps *especially* when we were.

Our general manager was a bigger-than-life guy named Bill Bolster. In an attempt to connect via the traditionally masculine avenue of sports, I mentioned baseball. But Bill didn't care much for baseball.

"I'll teach you how to play golf instead," he said. "It'll serve you far better than baseball."

Maybe. But the first time he took me to the golf range and I hit the ball, it ricocheted off a wall and hit me in the balls. I never hit another golf ball after that. And I'm pretty sure Bill understood.

When we took over KSDK, we inherited a station that was in last place in the ratings. Our sports department was the worst and Ron Jacober was part of that team. At the time, a big national story was about the St. Louis Cardinals team player Joaquin Andujar, who was implicated in cocaine use along with Pirates player Dave Parker. This was all going down while the Pirates were in town playing the Cardinals.

"Go down and stake out Parker's arrival to get an interview," I told our reporter, Ron. "Then get an interview with Andujar at Busch Stadium."

"No, I'd get my ass beat," Ron said.

"If you refuse, it would be considered insubordination," I warned.

But he still wouldn't go, so I sent a news reporter to cover it. Jacober's refusal would eventually lead to his dismissal a few months later. He was the perfect example of old school sports reporters who were such good friends with the team members that they couldn't cover stories about them.

Then there was Stan Stovall. He was our main anchor—a chiseled, good-looking man who had a penchant for bounty hunters and tough guys. And he was a weightlifter. But he decided to go to Philadelphia, so I had to replace him. We brought in someone considerably more intellectual and down-to-earth. That man was Huel Perkins.

At the time, Huel was a law student in Baton Rouge, Louisiana. He was also a young TV news anchor, but had viewed journalism as more of a fallback career in case lawyering didn't work out.

When Steve Antoniotti greenlighted it, we asked Huel if he would like to come work with us in St. Louis. His response was, "Probably not. I think I'll just stay in Louisiana and finish out law school. But just out of curiosity, what does it pay?"

When we told him the job paid between $60,000 and $100,000, he gave up law school right away and came directly to St. Louis. After all, he'd been making only $18,000 in Baton Rouge. It was one of the best decisions that Steve, Huel, and I would all make.

As we continued to clean house at KDSK, we also recognized that one of the best ways to boost ratings was to shake things up a bit. Even if it was one of the riskiest as well.

With that in mind, we did an exposé about "the brewery." That's how Anheuser-Busch was known in St. Louis. And it was a formidable entity. Going up against "the brewery" was a little like taunting the mafia. The other two major stations in town steered clear of them. So we knew we were playing with fire.

But it turns out that their relaxed policies about allowing workers to consume beer on the premises led to a worker getting into a serious accident that caused the deaths of several people. So we decided to take them on. Because it was the right thing to do.

I got a call from their PR firm telling me not to fuck with the brewery or I'd be out a job. This made me want to do the story all the more. In fact, I made a decision at that point, that if I couldn't do news the way I wanted to, I would allow myself to be fired.

Lucky for me, our station's top boss had a sense of justice and cared about the public. When I told him about the story, he asked: "Is your information on the brewery good? Is it reliable? And would you stake my career on it?"

I answered in the affirmative for all three.

"Good," he nodded. "Fuck them. And shove it up their ass."

We ended up doing a series of stories that caused them to change that policy. And I didn't lose my job over it, or get roughed up by beer thugs in a dark alley, either.

As KSDK started picking up steam, the competition over at KMOX—which later became KMOV—wasn't looking at us too kindly. In our highly competitive industry, it was a cardinal sin for management at the stations to fraternize.

One night, however, my boss and I were at Anthony's, a five-star restaurant in St. Louis. We noticed that rival bosses from KMOX were there as well. Feeling confident in all of the progress KSDK was making, my boss sent drinks to their table. These drinks were, of course, declined. That should have been the end of it, but of course, it wasn't.

My boss got up, walked over to the table and melted down on the guy. He looked him square in the eye and said loudly, "We are going to kick your ass into submission, mister." He added another graphic statement that everyone around us could hear. In the middle of this very classy restaurant with people at other tables watching aghast, I didn't know whether to be embarrassed or proud.

In the course of just one year, KSDK went from worst to first. We broke a lot of stories and won a lot of Emmy Awards.

For example, during the TWA hostage crisis in 1985, I took advantage of my relationship with Nabih Berri, who headed the Amal Movement in Lebanon, where he is now Speaker of the Parliament. Well before that in Detroit, I had met him on a story and saved his phone number. I told everyone in the newsroom I'd call him and nobody believed me. Next thing I know, we're getting exclusive phone interviews with him about the status of the hostages. When the hostages were eventually released, we flew to Boston and got exclusive interviews that even NBC Nightly News Anchor Tom Brokaw couldn't score.

Another riveting story happened in 1986. A woman who lived across the Mississippi River in Illinois claimed that a masked man came into her house, then kidnapped and murdered her daughter, Lorelei. A massive manhunt ensued shortly after that. But by this time, I'd been in the business long enough to feel that something was off with the mother. I didn't trust her and felt that she did it. So I sent a reporter to the news conference and told her to point-blank ask the woman if she killed her daughter. It was a calculated risk. And of course, the mother denied it.

Everyone thought the question was cold, insensitive, and horrible. I took a lot of slack for it. But my gut continued to tell me she was lying.

I wouldn't be in St. Louis long enough to see the case resolved. But three years later, the mother once again claimed that the same masked man came and took her six-week old daughter, Heather, and killed her too. That clinched it. They arrested this monster of a woman and put her away where she belonged.

My gut feeling, which had served me so well in the newsroom, had come through again. I was vindicated, in the most unfortunate way. But it did confirm that my gut is far more often correct than not.

A RACIST LABEL: "THE GARBAGE MEN"

"The garbage men."

That's what they were sometimes called in the private meetings held by white male management. And virtually every large city TV newsroom had one. Who were they? The young- to middle-aged Black males who were talented reporters, but were often hired merely to fill a quota during changing times in the industry and the country.

I was disgusted by this degrading label that often trapped these journalists at the bottom rungs of the on-air talent hierarchy. I thought, *If someone is good enough to be here, then they should be able to be assigned to cover any story.* That's not how it worked, though.

I worked in five different newsrooms. And whether I was in Detroit, Chicago, or St. Louis, it was virtually always the same. Black women were making inroads at the anchor desk—usually to sit beside an established white male. Beverly Payne and Doris Biscoe in Detroit were good examples. Similar talent placements were occurring in newsrooms throughout the country. But Black male anchors remained strangely absent. In fact, Black men in TV news were lacking altogether.

Meanwhile, in high-level newsroom editorial meetings, the white male management would ponder which stories they felt Black reporters "could handle." It was insulting and disgraceful. As a white male young pup in the industry at that time, I could listen, watch, and then try to impact change when I had the opportunity.

When I got to WBBM in 1981, we had a very good, soft-spoken reporter, Burleigh Hines, who has long since retired and passed away. I soon realized that he was always assigned the last—thus the least important—story, and he rarely covered any stories that led the newscast. And if he did, it was purely by accident.

After observing this for a few months, I felt that I had enough power as a mid-level manager to try to change this. So I recommended that we assign Hines to cover a more relevant story.

The bosses did not want to give Hines the responsibility or the opportunity to prove himself. Nor was effort made to help him improve. I suggested Hines for stories often; the bosses always said no. This troubled me deeply, and I felt obligated to tell Hines what was happening.

So one day I walked to the back of the newsroom and sat down with him. After some small talk, I asked: "How does it feel to be seen as 'the Garbage Man' in our newsroom?"

He looked at me inquisitively. "What do you mean?"

I told him that management above me believed it had good reasons to assign him the least important stories of the day.

"There have been times," I explained, "where I've suggested that you be assigned a specific story, but I always got shot down."

As this continued, I decided to work with Hines to coach him up.

"While you may never become the go-to guy," I said, "You can grow your game, get better, and be more of a factor in our coverage plan."

Hines did get better. He rose to the position, smiling and exuding pride. Still, he was never going to get the respect he deserved.

Another Black journalist was perceived and treated much the same way at WLS as Hines was at WBBM. Like Hines, this reporter would aim to please, but our rough-and-tumble management team made the relationship contentious. Though this reporter had a good voice and he could write, it didn't help that his work ethic was not the most motivated. And Black or white, I couldn't tolerate anybody just phoning it in. The truth is, I didn't like him, and he didn't like me.

One summer, a brutal heat wave struck Chicago. People were dying. So I called this reporter into my office and told him I wanted him to cover the story.

"But don't just go out and ask what people are doing to beat the heat," I advised. "Come up with something really strong. Find out what people who have no money are doing, for example. Just do something strong."

Early in the day before the report was supposed to air, I checked in with him. He said he was going to front the story at the lagoon in Lincoln Park. I wasn't sure how "strong" a story that would be. In terms of locations, it was pretty hackneyed. But I begrudgingly gave him the benefit of the doubt.

So the night of the broadcast, the camera panned to him.

"When I got to work this morning," he said, "my boss man told me to do a story on what people are doing to beat the heat." The boss, of course, was me.

He ran through some of the things people were doing. Pretty run-of-the-mill stuff. But then at the end of the story, he looked directly in the camera and said, "Mort, here's what I'm going to do. This one's for you."

Stripping down to his boxers, he jumped into the pond.

Now, this reporter—and everyone else at the studio—assumed I'd be mad. And they were nervous when he entered the building after the broadcast. But I stood up and applauded him. Then everyone gave him a standing ovation. Yeah, he'd been trying to piss me off. But it hadn't worked. In fact, it backfired. And he'd actually done a great story.

Twenty years later, this reporter called me. He told me he had hated me then, and that he still didn't like me. But he wanted to tell me that that particular story had changed him and his career for the better.

Sadly, many Black male journalists felt defeated. Their confidence suffered, even as they continued to grow as reporters.

Meanwhile, some maverick Black reporters used unconventional tactics that won acclaim. For example, Russ Ewing worked at NBC affiliate WMAQ-TV in Chicago and joined our team at ABC, WLS also in Chicago. He was legendary for asking fugitive felons—rapists, murderers, and armed robbers—to surrender to him, sometimes in the newsroom, but more often in a remote location, their home, on the street, or even in the cop shop. They complied, feeling it was safer surrendering to Ewing than the police. Ewing, who often carried a gun to work, would then escort them to the police stations. For this, Russ was different and he stood out. To this day Russ Ewing is the only reporter who ever worked for me who brought a piece to work with him each and every day.

REPORTER JOHN NOEL RISES TO GREATNESS IN AMERICA'S TOP TV MARKET

At KSDK in St. Louis, the management team was committed to helping everyone achieve his or her highest potential. This strategy involved mentoring and grooming our reporters to improve. I focused on helping John Noel. Even though he always came to work five minutes early and usually brought me an oatmeal cookie, his reporting skills were amateur.

This wasn't his fault, though. CBS News had hired John as a junior reporter to comply with an Affirmative Action policy that required employing a certain number of Black staff members. John was originally from Granada, and he was Black.

"I'll give you six months to improve," I told him, adding that keeping his job depended on his becoming a better reporter. To use a baseball analogy, my goal was to make John a singles hitter. He would, however, strike out most days.

I appreciated his spirit and determination, though. Plus, he'd overcome huge hurdles to get to KSDK—Affirmative Action aside. Growing up, John's family immigrated to New York. As a teenager, he was an addict who quit school and made a habit of holding people up at gunpoint. Then one day, he decided to clean up his act and join the military. From that point forward until the day he died, he never touched an ounce of alcohol or took a single drug. He also became proficient in the martial arts. Philosophically, John and I were aligned.

When I left KSDK to come to Detroit in 1988, I was in desperate need of others who bought into my philosophy. By that time, John had made himself into a singles hitter. So I brought him on. It wasn't long before he became a doubles hitter, and then after 10 years, a triples hitter.

When I was asked to leave WJBK, he didn't want to stay there without me. He wanted to return to New York—the country's biggest media market—and continue working in TV news. After he asked me to represent him as his talent agent, I got him a job in New York and I didn't ask for a contract from him. He was that special to me.

John Noel became a great reporter in New York—covering national and international stories. He was in the Major Leagues. Then one day he called me and said, "I had a seizure."

He died 16 months later—but worked every day of those 16 months, sure that he would beat the disease. In the days before his death, he called me while lying in bed. He was blind. In a weak voice, he said, "I'm going to beat this thing."

That was the last time I talked to him.

FEW SHATTERED THE BLACK CEILING IN NEWSROOMS

John was fortunate, because he had options to advance his career. That was not true for some Black men who had been in the industry longer than John.

Al Allen, whose real name is Andrew Long, was an older version of John and was at WJBK when I took it over. Al was unquestionably a good reporter, and describes his pioneering career as a Black journalist in his 2018 memoir, *We're Standing By*.

When I arrived at WJBK, I recognized that prior management had never given Al the opportunity to maximize his greatest potential. So, when I arrived, Al was the low man on the totem pole. I think talent like Al were hired for the sake of appearance, and management did nothing to foster their growth.

So, I had the same talk with Al as I'd had years earlier with Burleigh Hines in Chicago. Like Burleigh, Al had a great desire to be better.

And indeed, he accomplished so much during his trailblazing 50-year career in radio and TV. He covered Detroit's 1975 riot, the funeral procession for Rosa Parks in Washington, D.C., crimes, and scandals. And he became a beloved presence on the morning show, known for reporting live in snow storms to alert millions of viewers about what they needed to know each day.

Al persevered, and became a popular icon and local legend.

Another example was one of the rare Black male anchors—a rising star at WDIV in Detroit. But he simply had too many demons and we had to let him go. Reverend Jesse Jackson called and asked if we would give him a second opportunity. Wanting so much to see him succeed, we did so. But soon after, we had to let him go because the demons reappeared in the form of substance abuse. It was an addiction he just couldn't shake. It's a shame. He could have owned this town. He was that good.

Then there was Bob Bennett of CBS-owned WWJ-TV in Detroit, which later became the NBC affiliate, WDIV. Bob had been a political reporter, but was made into an early morning reporter who didn't make much impact.

Many more stories like this played. And all of them made me sad to watch.

Things have changed a lot over the years, but still not enough. Bill Proctor starred at WXYZ in Detroit as an investigative reporter. These days, outside of the business, Proctor works to get innocent, wrongly convicted men and women out of prison.

The question remains—was it different for women of color? I think management saw them as less threatening. And while things have changed over the years and management has become more diverse, it's still not enough.

THE LOVE BOAT IT WASN'T

Up until 1983, the fast life that was the natural by-product of the music and news industries had not been conducive to developing enduring romances for me. But that didn't stop me from getting in and out of serious relationships with women, a number of times. Because, why the hell not?

Those crazy, early, boozy years at WXYZ marked one of the times I got into a relationship I should have run away from. The young woman's name doesn't matter, but I met her on 8 Mile Road. On a national level, 8 Mile Road was made famous by the Eminem movie *8 Mile* in 2002. This was the first time many Americans understood the relevance of this eight-lane, divided road.

For those of us living in and around Detroit after the 1967 revolution and riots, 8 Mile Road has long been understood as the dividing line between Detroit and its northern suburbs. As white residents fled the city in 1967—in a mass exodus known as White Flight—they established themselves in neighborhoods north of this line. Black residents—whether by choice or financial necessity—stayed south of that line.

Until recently, 8 Mile was lined with controversial strip clubs, gas stations, a few restaurants, and plenty of prostitutes. If you were "walking 8 Mile," you were hooking. I was not into any of that, though. Cruising 8 Mile Road was just something to do back then. It provided interesting visuals while listening to Seger, Springsteen, and just killing time.

Anyhow, I was in my car and pulled up to a red light. I glanced over to my right and noticed a woman driving the car next to me. We made eye contact. It was electrifying!

But when the light turned green, she took off. Her car disappeared into traffic. Unwilling to surrender that overwhelming moment to fate, I was determined to find her. So, assuming she lived in one of the neighborhoods off 8 Mile, I drove around for 90 minutes until I found her car. I left my number and she was impressed, so she called me.

Soon we were dating, and eventually got married. It was the perfect starter marriage. She and I were both too young. And her parents were as nuts as mine were. It was a match made in hell from the get-go. We were married in December of 1977 and divorced in 1980. It's a miracle it lasted that long.

And of course, marriage and pending fatherhood brought me to Chicago in 1981. We married, and my wonderful son Jason was born in 1982. Unfortunately, I was still using cocaine heavily—even getting high with my wife's female friends. She began threatening to leave me, but I didn't really believe her.

Things got worse from there. And when I missed Jason's first birthday party because of a breaking news story—which now is inconceivable to me—we had a huge fight. When I came home from work the next day, she had cleared out everything from the house. EVERYTHING. I thought we'd been robbed. But she had taken Jason and moved in with her parents. She filed for divorce in 1983. It was clear, though, that our happy little home would never be of the white picket fence variety.

After that, I was only allowed to see Jason one day at a time. And I could never have him overnight. It was too painful. To deal with it, I kept myself so busy that I just never had enough time to be a big part of his life. It's not how I would handle it now. But hindsight is 20/20. And eventually, I would establish a relationship with Jason. By the time I moved to St. Louis, I flew to Chicago to see Jason, or had Jason flown to see me—at least once every month.

In August of 1983, I met Leslie and we married in April of 1984.

During this time, I was all about doing everything in a big way. So, we had our wedding in Italy. But this created a challenge because Italian law requires that an Italian official must notarize your divorce papers before you can marry in their country. So I mailed them to the mayor of Florence; he signed them and sent them back. Then we flew into Amsterdam and took a train to Florence. We were supposed to get married the next day, so we decided to go to the city hall to remind them of this.

It was at precisely this point that they informed us in the classic Italian way of yelling that the mayor had died and that the papers that were signed by the mayor were no longer valid. We had to wait three or four days to establish residency in the city of Florence. Then we went to the city hall to get married, and they said we needed five witnesses. Not knowing anybody in Italy, I found two Dutch couples and an Italian man out on the street who said they'd be witnesses. The wives of the Dutch couples thought for a little bit that we were attempting to shake them down.

We weren't, of course. And we've been married ever since.

AT THE TOP OF MY GAME

In 1988, I was flying high in St. Louis when I got an offer I couldn't refuse from Steve Antoniotti. He had moved to Detroit again a year earlier and he wanted me to step in and attempt to resuscitate a dying station there. So I returned to my hometown and inherited a newsroom at WJBK that was more than mildly reminiscent of the set from *One Flew Over the Cuckoo's Nest*. This included untalented people working in what was mostly a country club atmosphere.

For example, I inherited a weather guy who acted like he owned the station. Not only was he arrogant and cocky, he literally acted as if he could do anything he wanted. When it came to my attention that he was actually giving private martial arts lessons in the building at night between newscasts, I brought him into my office and confronted him. He admitted that he was doing this, but saw nothing wrong with it.

"You have to stop the classes immediately," I said.

Always hungry for confrontation, he attempted to verbally joust about it and lost—at which point he went into one of the station bathrooms, ripped a toilet out of the wall, and damaged the sink.

I fired him the next day. I would have let him go eventually though, because honestly, he was a below-average talent who didn't belong in a major market.

Coincidentally, he would leave WJBK to go to WBBM, where

he'd also be fired not too long after. He'd end up repeating this poor behavior throughout his career, until there was no more career of which to speak.

WJBK wasn't my first time working with Antoniotti. We'd worked together in the late 1970s and early 1980s in Detroit. He'd also been one of the guys who attempted to bring me to KNBC in Los Angeles, but I'd turned him down. He even surfaced in St. Louis and hired me there. And so now here I was working with him in Detroit again.

Having pulled a couple of stations from near extinction, I knew that one of my first orders of business at WJBK was to stress the importance of being competitive. I told Steve that we needed a satellite truck.

The way Steve looked at me, I might as well have asked for 10, because we couldn't even afford one. I resigned myself to the fact that this wasn't going to happen any time soon. If ever. So I put it on the back burner.

Meanwhile, I got right to work, offering Jerry Stanecki a job at the station. He'd long been fired from Channel 7 in part due to budget, and in part because he was incorrigible. I knew this already and didn't let it deter me. I wanted to reinvent the News Hawk and thought he was just the guy to do it. But another aspect of Stanecki was that he really didn't want to work all that hard. And things became especially difficult when Jerry requested he work from home because he no longer wanted to come to the station. This was not something we could reconcile, and he eventually left. We managed to stay friends, though. Not too long after that, I took him to lunch one day. When he found out I was paying, he got an order to go, too. That gives you a picture of what Stanecki was like.

Another person who didn't work out so great was the late Joe Glover. Before I came to WJBK, Steve Antoniotti told me he was going to hire Glover. I told him that bringing in Glover, who had worked at WJBK previously, was not a good idea. But it fell on deaf ears.

My issues with Glover were not personal. In fact, I liked the guy. I'd even mentored his daughter. But at the time, he was coming out of a difficult marriage and had been accused of putting a snake in his wife's underwear drawer while they were going through the divorce. It wasn't necessarily the drama surrounding him that was the problem, though.

Glover was actually a pretty relaxed guy. A bit too relaxed at times. For example, the night that the Pan Am Flight 103 en route to Detroit was bombed over Lockerbie, Scotland, I needed Joe to get on the flash cam in the newsroom right away. When I walked over to his office, he was lounging around in sweats and an undershirt. I admonished him, telling him he needed to get more serious. It didn't do much, though.

Our relationship continued to deteriorate and hit a low point when I told him he could only have one hour for dinner—like everybody else. I also prohibited him from going at the same time as our female anchor, so there'd always be one anchor there for breaking news. Apparently, he didn't take too kindly to these rules and demonstrated it by throwing a chair at me. He was suspended; I fired him shortly thereafter.

Under the category of "silver linings," Glover's departure meant that I was able to promote Huel Perkins to a higher position.

"I'm going to double your salary," I told Huel.

"For that money," he said, "I'll do the morning, the noon, the four, the five, the six, the ten, and the eleven!"

I never had any regrets about Huel. And I can honestly say I've never worked with another news person who was more socially conscious and cared more about his fellow workers and citizens than Huel.

In fact, one day in the Oak Room at WJBK, we had a group of young Black girls and boys from Detroit schools. Huel gave them a speech about the importance of education. He was sincere and his words were captivating. Most of the students seemed legitimately interested.

When he got to the end of the hour or so presentation, one student raised her hand and asked him for an autograph.

"No!" he said sharply. "No autographs for anyone here today!"

The students were taken aback until Huel softened.

"No autographs," he began, the beginnings of a smile on his lips, "UNLESS you take the time to write me a letter and ask me for it. You see, writing is so important. It will get you places and open doors."

He went on to stress the importance of vocabulary and writing.

"If you all write me a letter, I'll send you each an autograph," he said. And for the students who wrote him letters, he did just that.

Huel touched those young people that day and his words touched me.

HEARING THE TRUTH FROM A RESPECTED COLLEAGUE

One of the greatest managers who ever worked for me was Tom Bell, who just happens to be the father of actress Kristen Bell. I was lucky enough to inherit him at WJBK.

Tom walked around with a legal pad and had the strange habit of writing from the bottom up. He was incredibly efficient and dependable.

"Done," he announced when he finished an assignment. This was not the case with many others, but when Tom said it, I knew it was true.

I trusted his word; he had been my "spy" at WJBK before I arrived, keeping me abreast of what was messed up and what needed fixing.

I thought he was a good friend. But after Tom left WJBK to become the news director at WWJ News Radio 950, I heard through the grapevine that he'd told a coworker there that he'd never really liked me. I have to admit that it really hurt. So I steered clear of him for a couple of years. But then one day I decided to ask him about it.

He admitted saying that, adding that he understood why I had been "a hardass" while trying to drastically improve the station. But this made me wonder, *Had I been too hard on others there, too?* As I pondered this, I knew that I had done what was necessary to ensure the station's survival. In the end, Tom and I did become great friends. He even threw me a surprise party for my 40th birthday.

WILD STORIES FROM THE NEWSFRONT

In June of 1990, my former higher school classmate Geoffrey Fieger called me. He was now an attorney, like his father, who had been our lawyer at the Grande. Anyhow, Geoffrey was calling to say he was with an eccentric older guy who had just "offed" a woman in Holly, a small town 55 miles northwest of Detroit.

"What are you talking about?" I asked.

"It was a woman from Portland (Oregon) with Alzheimer's who wanted to die. And this guy made that possible."

That guy was Dr. Jack Kevorkian and he'd just performed assisted suicide. Because Geoffrey and I had that connection, he only called me. No other media had the information and we got exclusive coverage of the story. WJBK was starting to be seriously recognized.

In spite of how things were looking up at WJBK, Detroit as a city was still struggling with its bad reputation for a high crime rate, poverty, and racial division. Things came to a head one year during the Independence Day Fireworks when two teenage Black women beat up two white women from Dearborn. It made national news. And you can bet it didn't do much to boost Detroit's reputation.

The next day, a friend of mine who was a private investigator, called and told me he had video of the incident. He was willing to give it to me as long as I didn't reveal where I got it. He brought me the video and we looked at it. We ran the story.

When the two women were arraigned in court, the defense attorneys demanded that we turn over the identity of the guy who shot the video. I refused. They threatened to hold me in contempt of court and throw me in jail. Fortunately, our attorney at Channel 2, Henry Saad, successfully argued our position and we never revealed it. This from a guy who claimed to never watch TV news and didn't even own a TV.

We took a lot of heat for it, though. But it helped us grow our name, and we protected our source; to this day, nobody ever managed to get that video.

When Detroit Mayor Coleman Young was in office, we never experienced a dull moment. Young was a self-described street-fighter. He was also a race baiter, which—as strange as it may sound—was what the city needed at that time.

Detroit had become predominantly Black, yet its police department was almost entirely white. Because of this, Black residents suffered unfairly for years at the hands of many racist cops. This isn't to say that all, or even the majority, of the white police officers were racist. But it was definitely a big problem.

Young was a vocal and verbose figure who never missed a moment to speak his mind. Shortly after he was elected as the city's first Black mayor in 1974, he publicly suggested that "whitey hit 8 Mile Road." Unfortunately, because Young was known to say controversial things, this was taken out of context. In this case, he was referring to white criminals, and that he wanted them to leave Detroit. To this day, people recall this statement out of context, as if he were telling all white people to leave the city.

Even so, and with all due respect, Mayor Young's statements were often delivered with a lot of hot air. For example, one October night during the late 1980s, the blowhard mayor called me.

As soon as I said, "Hello," he launched into one of his standard tirades.

"What the fuck is so motherfucking sacrosanct about running old video of the Devil's Night fires?" he yelled.

This was during Detroit's troubled years when arsonists torched hundreds of abandoned houses and buildings on October 30, also known as Devil's Night. Anywhere between 500 and 800 fires blazed on this night before Halloween, putting residents in danger. Every year, we ran footage of fires from previous years to remind viewers of what to expect. The problem was so bad, TV crews from Japan and elsewhere around the world came to capture Detroit burning on camera.

So when Mayor Young called me, the answer seemed clear.

"Obviously it's in a couple of days," I snapped back, irritated by yet another of his rants. "And the fact that they're burning your city down is newsworthy."

"They're not burning it down right now," he countered. "And when you show these motherfuckin' videos of past fires, it just puts ideas in their heads to do it again this year!"

I hated having to agree with him, but he was right. We did not need to rehash this footage year after year and, in a sense, glorify it.

"Alright," I agreed. "I get it. So here's the deal. We won't run any footage from previous years' fires. But if any fires start burning tonight or tomorrow or whenever, it's news. And we will run them."

Young was satisfied.

I can't say the same for my newsroom when I issued an edict saying we would not air any footage from previous years' fires. I also said we would no longer refer to them as Devil's Night fires, but rather pre-Halloween fires.

Some of the people in my newsroom reported this fact to the *Detroit Free Press*, which published an article claiming that I was in bed with the mayor. This was bullshit. Especially since I'd been one of his biggest critics. Regardless of my feelings toward the mayor, though, he was right.

This was one of those rare opportunities in local news where I got the chance to take a step back and think about the decision I was making, and how it would impact the community. I refused to feel bad about it. If I had the chance to do it over again, I'd do it exactly the same way.

Because of his hot-tempered communication style, many local journalists joked that it was hard to believe much of what came out of Coleman Young's office. Some people in the media believed that his press secretary, Bob Berg, was essentially hired to lie for the mayor, and that he actually made sport of lying. In fact, on the night of Coleman Young's death, I had a source at the Wayne County morgue who verified that the mayor had died. Even then, Bob refused to play along—unwilling to confirm the mayor's death.

It's a stark change to the Detroit mayor's office today.

In my continued attempts to build a strong team at WJBK, I hired Rich Fisher away from WXYZ in August of 1990. I offered him about three million dollars for five years. But sometimes things just aren't meant to be. Rich was a great communicator. He gave us a name and a lot of credibility. But to no fault of his own, he just wasn't a great fit at WJBK. The fact that he seemed to perpetually dwell in Bill Bonds' shadow didn't help matters. It seemed, at least subconsciously, that Rich was always trying to be the legendary character that Bill was. As a result, many people only ever saw him as a wanna-be.

Rich remained at WJBK until shortly after I departed in the late 1990s. After that, he worked for a time at WKBD-TV, the CW-owned Channel 50, and then on the fringes of the industry. Rich lost a brutal battle with esophageal cancer in March of 2017 and I, along with his sons and daughters, were at his side during the last days.

A few years later, it was obvious that we desperately needed more strong females at Channel 2. Though we had quite a few women at the time, none could really break through as a leading anchor. The solution? Entice either Diana Lewis from WXYZ or Carmen Harlan from WDIV. Carmen was available. So we offered her three million dollars over a period of time. We met with her, her attorney, and her agent several times, and finally settled on an agreement.

We met at the Skyline Club in Southfield to seal the deal. Then out of the blue, her lawyer got up to take a phone call, came back, and whispered in her agent's ear.

After a moment of silence, her agent looked up at me and said, "We reject your offer. Carmen is staying at WDIV."

And that was that.

Carmen hadn't been making even remotely that kind of money at WDIV, so our offer must have inspired them to offer her a big raise. I thought maybe she'd someday thank me for indirectly making that happen. But she never did.

That's the news business for you. Pretty funny.

Murray Feldman was a different story, though.

I've always said, "He's one of those guys who, when he walked into my office, I would sit in my chair and listen." Usually when people walked in, I'd get up, so that they couldn't sit down and start complaining. But not Murray.

I always likened Murray Feldman to Al Kaline, the Detroit Tigers Hall of Fame Right Fielder. When Kaline complained about a bad call, he was almost always right. If Murray came in with a *kvetch* (that's Yiddish for a complaint)—which was rarely—it was usually well-warranted. I respect Murray and consider him the most honorable man I worked with during my 20 years in newsrooms and my nearly 40 years in the TV news business.

During my tenure at WJBK, at least one incredibly talented but sometimes challenging employee was on the payroll. That was sports anchor Eli Zaret.

Eli had been successful on FM radio. With a raspy voice and while not exactly a "face for radio," he did have an interesting look. He wasn't always liked among his peers. But I liked him and thought he was a good guy. At one point, we decided to pair up Eli with ex-Tiger Denny McClain, who had been in and out of jail for looting the pension fund for a company he owned up north. But he'd also been charged with making threats of bodily harm and intimidation. That landed him jail at least a few times.

Anyhow, we called it the Eli and Denny Show. It had good ratings—for a Sunday morning. Which isn't saying a whole lot. Because getting good ratings on a Sunday morning doesn't really give you bragging rights.

Eli and Denny didn't realize this. They came into my office one day to show me the ratings and to remind me they were only being paid $500 per show. Then they had the nerve to demand twice that amount for each show. So we called their bluff and canceled the show. Denny looked at me with an exasperated expression that said something to the effect of "I'm fucking Denny McClain."

"Get out," I said.

Honestly, I don't think Eli was surprised at all.

I knew that being a good manager meant not always being liked. In fact, I was downright hated sometimes. I was okay with this, though. I had to be.

Eli, on the other hand, was not. And his desire to be liked didn't foster the skills needed to be a good manager. A few sports people who worked for him essentially ran roughshod in the sports department.

"You need to get a handle on them," I often warned him. Otherwise, he'd risk becoming a fat cat without a job.

The other thing that made Eli a bit of a wild card was his temper. For example, he was always frustrated at the crappy state of our equipment. One day he was doing a live report from Tiger Stadium. I always insisted the crews set up monitors, so that the talent could see what was going on in front of them. On that given day, the monitor didn't work. During a commercial break, Eli took the monitor, threw it, then smashed what was left of it. I understood his frustration, and even agreed with his action. Even so, I had to suspend him.

Overall though, Eli was a true professional and one of the best sports guys I've ever worked with.

AN UNFORTUNATE REALITY: FEMALE FAVORS

In as much as broadcasting was tough for anyone who wasn't white, it was equally harsh for women.

One evening around midnight, an intern called me at home to report that a lot of noise was coming from the office of a news anchor.

"Did you knock on the door and see what's going on?" I asked.

"Yeah," she said. "But nobody answered."

I sighed and rubbed my eyes. The station was only three miles away, but I didn't want to have to go there. "Try again," I said.

"Hold on," she said. I heard some shuffling and other unidentifiable sounds over the line. Then she came back on. "Still no answer."

So I got dressed and drove to the station. I knocked on the anchor's office door and demanded I be allowed in. What I saw disgusted me. The anchor and an intern where having sex on a desk. Liquor bottles were everywhere, and the whole scene was bizarre.

I fired the intern on the spot. If it were today, the news anchor would have (and should have) been fired as well. Instead, the anchor was merely suspended.

A different twist on this dynamic occurred with a female reporter. When music legend Del Shannon killed himself in California, I knew he was from Michigan. It was a big story that we needed to cover, and we needed something colorful. I had a reporter who I thought would be perfect to cover the story. This reporter was a go-getter and a gifted writer to boot. And she understood what a good story was.

So I sent her to Coopersville, Michigan, where he grew up, to cover the story. When she returned and it aired, people were blown away by how good her story was—especially because she had known nothing about Del Shannon.

What made (and continues to make) broadcasting a difficult industry for women is the sexual component. In other words, the whole idea that getting ahead will require certain "favors" be rendered. I've always found this deplorable. But it's deeply entrenched in the culture.

When it came time for this reporter to move to another state, I was thrilled for her success and glad we'd become friends. We got together for a few celebratory drinks. Then she invited me up to her room. I figured she wanted to say goodbye in a more private space. But when we got to her room, she told me how thankful she was that I'd taken a chance on her when I hired her. And now she wanted to pay me back.

"I'm flattered," I said, "but I don't do that."

My response was so outside of her realm of thinking that she was, I believe, insulted. After that night, she never returned my calls or emails.

I always thought we'd been friends. I was sad to later find out that this former WJBK reporter had passed away.

LEADING COVERAGE ON AN INTERNATIONAL STORY

In terms of notoriety, the biggest story of my career was the Tonya Harding/Nancy Kerrigan attack. The story made international and national headlines.

It's what came later that made this story so unbelievable, so crazy, so bizarre that Tanya Harding's gang of cretins had actually plotted to whack Olympic figure skater Nancy Kerrigan in the knees with a baton during a competition at Detroit's Cobo Hall in January of 1994.

As the drama unfolded, Detroit Police Chief Ike McKinnon remained my source—and I mean on every aspect of the story. I assigned outstanding investigative reporter Scott Lewis as the primary talent on this story. Scott killed it! Together, we won some pretty impressive awards for our work.

The conspiracy with this group included credit card records, phone records… you name it, we had it. In national and international media circles, no one could figure out how this CBS affiliate in Detroit—even though the incident occurred there—was breaking news on the case before every station and every network. We were beating our competition so dramatically that I got a call from CBS News (since we were a CBS affiliate) asking about how we were getting our information. Of course, I never told. Jealous, typically, as the networks were at that time of locally-owned and operated affiliates, I was challenged on the veracity of the story.

I said, "Fine. Don't fuckin' use our story."

So after CBS rejected our story, I turned around and gave the story to NBC. In retrospect, I probably shouldn't have done that. I wanted the story to get out on the national level, though. Soon I was being interviewed by *The Wall Street Journal*, *The New York Times*, and other national and regional print and radio publications who were interested in the story.

Meanwhile, because WJBK was a locally-owned station, we continued to cover the story in Detroit. And we led the way from start to finish. All of which further infuriated the vice president of news for CBS.

It's funny. I never imagined that the story of a skater getting attacked would become an international spectacle. I thought it would just be another story about how rough things were in Detroit. But the saga and all the mystery and intrigue surrounding it just kept growing and growing.

In 1995, our coverage won an Emmy Award and was submitted and nominated for many other honors. Yet while nominations were made and celebrations ensued, the whole event had a bittersweet note for me. Just before I won the Emmy, my dear friend Nelson Burg succumbed to cancer.

While I don't consider this story the most important one of my career, it was certainly the biggest.

Thanks, Tonya. The gift that keeps on giving.

MAYOR ARCHER BRINGS HONESTY AND INTEGRITY TO REVITALIZE THE CITY

When Mayor Dennis Archer was elected in 1994, he brought an honesty and integrity to city hall that had been lacking during Young's years. For as much trouble as Coleman Young caused, Dennis Archer was his polar opposite. Archer was truly a breath of fresh air after Young's 20-year reign.

Dennis, as he asked me to call him time and time again, was honest as the day is long. Born in Detroit, he moved with his family to rural Cassopolis, Michigan when he was five. The home lacked running water, but Archer's parents instilled in him the importance of education and a strong work ethic. At eight years old, he began working as a golf caddy, and later worked his way through Western Michigan University, where he earned a bachelor's degree in Education. He returned to Detroit to work as a teacher for disabled children in the Detroit Public Schools system.

Then he earned his law degree and practiced as a trial lawyer, teaching as an associate professor at his alma mater, the Detroit College of Law, and as an adjunct professor at Wayne State University Law School. In 1986, he was appointed to the Michigan Supreme Court, but stepped down in 1990. In 1994, he succeeded Young.

His honesty didn't make him the best politician, though. Still, during his campaign, he and his supporters had good access to WJBK where I was the News Director. Dennis was running against Sharon McPhail, who was tough as nails, if not the best person. One night at the station, she called him "baldy" on the air. A tiff ensued, and eventually spilled into my office. It was a case of classy versus the classless. After McPhail and her handlers left, we were left shaking our heads.

Sometime later, after I left WJBK, I was building my agent business while working in media training and crisis management. During this time, I was meeting with Mayor Archer—whose former Police Chief Ike McKinnon was now the deputy mayor. When I walked into the mayor's office, rain pelted the window and Dennis looked tired and worn.

"How 'ya doing?" I asked.

He looked straight at me and shook his head. Then he explained that the Young administration had left a legacy of political patronage that proved challenging. He would later describe in his 2017 memoir, *Let The Future Begin*, how he inherited a plethora of difficult circumstances in city management.

When I left his office on that gray and rainy afternoon, I felt certain that Dennis Archer would not seek another term as mayor. He was just too classy, too wise, too smart, and too honest for a city that was so corrupt and so far gone. Sure enough, he decided not to run again. That fact alone was disappointing. As far as mayors though, the worst was yet to come.

CLASHING WITH STATION LEADERSHIP

As WJBK started getting back on its feet again, Steve Antoniotti was eventually let go. Ratings continued to struggle and corporate wasn't seeing the results they wanted. As new management joined the station, I had a hunch that things might get challenging. Even so, this meant another opportunity to rally for a satellite truck.

And another opportunity, it turned out, for them to say, no way.

But not having a truck would eventually bite us in the ass. On the day of the Oklahoma City bombings in 1995, a connection was made to northern Michigan. The other local stations quickly got up there to cover the story. But not us.

So when the general manager came down the hall, seething and screaming at me about why we couldn't go live, I explained it was because he had told me we couldn't afford a satellite truck. End of conversation. He went off, angrily mumbling. As time went on, my relationship with management became increasingly difficult.

During this time, I attended a station party at the outdoor concert venue, Pine Knob, with my wife, a manager, and an anchor's wife; her husband would join us after he anchored the evening news. Inside a private courtyard, the manager pulled me aside and said of the anchor, "He's sorta a zero, right?"

Taken aback, I said, "He's a great friend and an excellent news anchor."

Then he commented that the anchor's wife was just a trophy wife.

Not sure where he was coming from, I told him, "I don't see it that way, and she's a good friend of mine."

Then he said, "Well, do you think I could fuck her?"

By this time, I decided that this man was the worst kind of sexist and that we would not get along. "Only if you ask her husband," I told him.

He walked away, shaking his head.

I also told the anchor, and he was furious.

Over time, I got sick and tired of sexist comments in the workplace. One day, my assistant and I attended a meeting with a high-ranking manager and two executives whom I viewed as "yes" people who towed the company line. We were talking ratings, which continued to be a great challenge.

By now we had an excellent product with incredible talent and I had a great management team. But we still had a lot going against us. Channel 7 was very strong—even after the Bill Bonds years, before the station took a major dive. And WDIV had remained—and does so to this day—consistent.

"What do you think we need to do to be number one?" the manager asked.

I talked about breaking habits, doing news pallet promotions, and being competitive on all fronts.

"Fuck that," he said, rolling his eyes. "What we need to do is have our anchor take her blouse off and put her big breasts on the anchor desk." The woman was a young and talented Black female anchor whom I had hired from a smaller market.

Much to my dismay, the two executives laughed.

"That's not funny," I said, then turned to my assistant. "We're leaving." Back in my office, I immediately called corporate. They began an investigation shortly thereafter. I can't say I'm solely responsible, but that manager was fired a short time later.

On a positive note, the anchor is now doing well as an anchor in one of America's biggest news towns.

GOING FROM BAD TO WORSE

That manager was perhaps the worst guy with whom I ever worked.

But I believed that his replacement was out for blood. Mine, specifically. In fact, I felt like I had a bullseye on my back.

He may have had other reasons for this strong dislike, but I suspect that he somehow associated me with a career setback years before. Back then, he was very successful, but my opinion was that he was untrustworthy and talked out of both sides of his mouth. With him now at the helm, it was clear that he was seeking revenge.

In my nearly 20 years in the news business, I received only one negative note. It was well deserved—for something stupid and immature—that I did way back during the 1970s. I had not even been in the business three years when the behind-the-scenes people at the station were considering going on strike. Anger was brewing over money, comp days, and vacation. I seriously thought that AFTRA Union leadership was going to pull the pin from the grenade.

We ultimately voted against it, but I decided, as a joke, to phone the on-call manager and tell him we didn't.

"Bob," I said, "we are going on strike and you better let the bosses know." It seemed amusing to me at the time.

The problem was, even though I'd also let an underling know that we were kidding, it turned out that word never made it back to management. When they found out what I'd done, corporate was advised and the shit hit the fan. I absorbed the wrath of my boss, when it was discovered that I was behind this childish prank.

"Ya know, for a smart guy and a great newsman," he yelled, "you sure did something stupid!" Honestly, I should have been fired. And I felt horrible that I'd let my boss down. I'd certainly learned my lesson.

Yet here it was 17 years later and all of a sudden, a top boss is doling out negative memos about me like they're going out of style. In just 30 days, he wrote 21 negative memos about me. He accused me of everything from lack of judgment in deploying news crews, to utter incompetence. He even tried to get Murray Feldman to turn against me. (Murray told me.)

During this same period, I was deeply disturbed by comments amongst colleagues that struck me as homophobic and racist. One manager referred to a staff member as "that fag," then added, "You have a lot of fags in the newsroom. I don't mind one or two, but I don't want a whole room of them."

Another time, an executive made an offensive comment about the hairstyle of a Black male on-air talent.

I called corporate. But this time, I'd gone to the well one too many times; I had an inkling that they weren't going to take my side again. A week later, I was called by HR. They said it wasn't working out and management wanted me to leave. They offered a buy-out that I didn't accept and told them that I wanted a year's salary.

They said they would negotiate, but meanwhile, I had to go. So I was ushered out of the building and let go.

The morning after, I violated one of my own rules: *always be vigilant when talking to a broadcaster*. The morning DJ on the country station called me. He said he was sorry to hear I'd left WJBK. I clarified by telling him that I hadn't left, but rather had been ushered from the station like a common criminal. I assumed that the DJ was reaching out to me. I never imagined he had me on the air. But he did. And I'd just made a serious mistake.

Fox withdrew the monetary offer they'd put on the table to buy me out. I had to start from scratch. It took a year and an attorney, but I did eventually get the money they offered me.

Yeah, it was a tactical error on my part. But I did feel I was ushered out like a common criminal after all the good work I'd done, bringing the station back to life.

And I was, once again, back to page one.

THE STORIES THAT REALLY MATTERED

It's sad to say, but broadcasting largely focuses on stories that will generate ratings. In my career—like most in TV news—many of those stories involved rapes, murders, breaking and entering, and armed robberies. What's worse, if the rapes or murders were of a domestic variety, they didn't make the cut. Neither did suicides. I guess stories that hit too close to home just didn't garner the viewership.

As for the negative news stories that did make it to the screen, I truly felt I was doing more than just covering them—by giving the audience something they couldn't get anywhere else.

I'm fortunate to really enjoy people, because I thrive on talking to random strangers. Many times, these random strangers have become friends. In the news business, you can't put a price on having friends "in the right places."

For example, one of the biggest stories out of the courts in the history of Chicago in the early 1980s was Operation Greylord. This was an investigation conducted jointly by the FBI, the IRS Criminal Investigation Division, the US Postal Inspection Service, the Chicago PD Internal Affairs Division, and the Illinois State Police into corruption in the judiciary of Cook County in the Chicago jurisdiction.

Two local courts and two Illinois attorneys agreed to operate undercover, as well as numerous FBI agents and cooperating local law enforcement officers. In addition, Assistant State's Attorney Terrence

Hake went undercover in the Criminal Division of the Cook County Circuit Court. Hake had complained about the bribery and corruption in the Murder and Sexual Assault preliminary hearing courtroom in Chicago. The FBI and US Attorney's Office learned of his complaint and recruited him to pose as a corrupt prosecutor, then later as a bribe-paying criminal defense attorney.

A source in the US Attorney's office was a friend of mine and he was able to give me this information ahead of the rest of the media. I went to my boss Bill Applegate at WLS in Chicago and shared what my friend had given me.

He gave me a dead serious look. "In terms of accuracy, are you willing to place your career on the line?"

I had the utmost confidence in my friend, so without missing a beat I said, "Absolutely."

Once he was satisfied that my source was good, we broke the story. It was huge in Chicago, and had both local and national repercussions. More than 92 federal officials were investigated, indicted, thrown off the bench, and even sent to prison—along with some attorneys.

Another amazing story while I was at ABC in Chicago was in 1983 when an Air Canada flight had to make an emergency landing in Cincinnati. During flight, a fire started behind the lavatory and spread between the outer skin and the inner panels. The plane began filling with toxic smoke. The fire also burned through electrical cables that disabled most of the instrumentation in the cockpit.

Ninety seconds after the plane landed, the doors were opened. The heat of the fire in combination with the fresh oxygen from the open exit doors created dangerous flashover conditions. The plane's interior was immediately engulfed in flames—killing 23 passengers who had not yet evacuated.

My source at the Federal Aviation Administration provided me with these grim but crucial facts. But the network newscasts were reporting there were few or no injuries. Even in my own building, ABC nationally was reporting that.

But our local news was reporting otherwise with the data we had. In other words, we were reporting the facts and not fake news. This underscores the importance of having impeccable sources. Especially now, when a lot of bad information is getting rolled out as factual.

Crazy as it is, this same FAA source was also on the phone with me years earlier when I was back in Detroit when a plane went down in Chicago and he said, "I gotta go, a plane just went down." It was quite a coincidence.

At KSDK in St. Louis, I was involved in putting the kibosh on a gay male prostitution ring. At the time, I was good friends with two cops who told me they were having big problems in one of the parks. So we put wires on them and sent them into the park. I don't recall if we cleared this with the police department or if we were working with our own unique brand of vigilantism. Either way, we did it.

One of the cops went into the bathroom and got someone to solicit sex from him. A man approached him and said he was looking to get "sucked and fucked."

The cop pulled out his handcuffs and said, "Well, you got one of them. You just got fucked."

It wasn't always about giving the audience something unique, though. Sometimes, stories moved me in other ways that made me want to get involved on a deeper level. I wanted to make a difference.

One of those stories was in 1979 when I was brand new to the business. At the time, prostitutes were being kidnapped, raped, and murdered. The assailant left his "mark" by putting palm leaves on the victims' bodies.

The story didn't get much coverage, though. The victims were prostitutes and therefore considered second-class citizens. But we believed a cover-up was happening. The Republican National Convention was coming to Detroit the following year, so it was believed that Coleman Young wanted to keep the story under wraps.

So much for that.

Although I was only two years in the business, I'd learned the value of having sources. One was Audrey Martini, Lieutenant in Charge of the Sex Crimes Unit. She was horrified by what was happening to these women. And she was just as irritated that the men in homicide didn't seem to care. She was the one who told me a cover-up was happening, so we started reporting about the "bus stop rapist murderer."

Then the story really blew up when a woman called the WXYZ assignment desk—where I happened to be that day—and told me that she had been a victim. She survived by playing dead until he left. Unlike most of the other women who were Black, she was white. She had dark marks under her eyes and ligature marks on her neck that indicated someone had attempted to strangle her.

On my urging, she went to the police and met with the head of homicide. The whole venture was pointless, though. He sent her away because neither he, nor the rest of the police, believed her.

So I went to Kathryn Kiefer, a female reporter who worked for me and whom I highly respected. I told her what was happening. We decided to collaborate on a series of stories about these prostitutes who were being raped and murdered.

Kathryn invited the woman to tell her story on the air. She described the crime, how she faked her death, and how when she went to police, they turned her away. Of course, this didn't go over too well with the police or the mayor's office.

The Detroit Police Department immediately put out a notification and sent it by fax to all the stations that Kathryn and I and Channel 7 were engaged in deceptive practices, and that no one should talk to us. Kathryn and I were sure we would get fired.

Not only were we not fired, but the general manager of the station, Jeanne Findlater, put out a news release that supported us while criticizing the Detroit Police Department. Although we can't say with certainty that it was all our doing, but the head of homicide was forced to retire a short time later.

It would be quite a few years before the man, Carl Watts, was caught and dubbed "The Sunday Morning Slasher."

Another story was about Viola Liuzzo, a white woman killed during the Civil Rights Movement. The Michigan mother of five was murdered along with two Black men while on a freedom fighting mission in 1965 in Selma, Alabama. Her murderers were Ku Klux Klan members.

J. Edgar Hoover was the head of the FBI at the time and served only to besmirch Liuzzo's image. He was determined to portray her as a whore who just wanted to have sex with Black men. Her case was sealed for years until her family sued the FBI during the late 1970s. At Channel 7, we did news stories to try to force those files unsealed. And finally, the family won the case to open them.

I built a relationship with Viola's children that continues today. Her murder put a tremendous strain on the family, and inspired her son, Tony Jr., to lecture on civil rights.

Then there was the child pornography investigation in St. Louis in 1987 of a motor cycle gang that nearly got me killed.

We had infiltrated a child pornography group along with the county and state police. We were buying the pornography, then turning it over to the authorities. I was fearless (or stupid) at the time, so at the end of the story, I put on a wireless mic and went into an adult book store in South St. Louis. It was very clear that the motorcycle gang knew I was on to them. They surrounded me and were about to assault me with a broken beer bottle—one they'd broken expressly for that purpose. When I walked in the final day to make a buy, I had a crew and the police outside. At that point, our crew and the police came in and saved me from what was sure to be an assault—maybe worse.

An incredible moment, but at least we were able to be a part of what put these guys in jail.

On another occasion in St. Louis, we infiltrated a traveling magazine group that was actually a human trafficking ring. Groups of young men led by an unscrupulous manager would usually have one young woman with them; she would be forced to have sex and be otherwise abused. The women had usually been solicited from bus stations or other places where wayward young women ended up. The men promised them work, but enslaved them instead. Part of the initiation for the men was to gang rape the woman at a certain point.

The "magazine" paid these males in their teens or early 20s not much more than a few dollars a day, and provided crappy food and modest shelter. But it was usually just an ongoing party. Some of the women who were lured in had no idea what was in store. Others were so downtrodden; they simply didn't care.

So we went to one of my producers, who'd worked for me in Chicago, and asked her if she'd be willing to go undercover to get these guys. Never one to miss the opportunity to cover a good story, she was game—in spite of (or maybe because of) the risk involved. Although she was 28, our producer could easily pass for 16.

We followed the group and often stayed in the same hotel. During our last week, we were staying at Travelodge in Wichita, Kansas. I was out to breakfast at a place called Pot Belly's and I had a big briefcase phone with me. One of the guys in the magazine group asked me if I was a cop. I told him no.

"Seems like I keep fuckin' seeing you everywhere," he said. "So you better disappear." Then he shoved me and hit me, right there in the restaurant.

I hit him in the side of the head with that enormous phone. That was enough to convince him that I wasn't going to be any sort of problem for him.

The night that the rape was to take place, we were set up in the room next to our producer's. She had a wireless mic. At some point, she went into the bathroom and said, "You can come in now." And we did—alongside the police—with the cameras rolling. I'm proud of this story—even though it involved a lot of risk. Especially for our producer.

During the late 70s, I worked with Jerry Stanecki—who was known as the "Newshawk"—on an investigation that infuriated a prominent businessman so much, he demanded that the station fire us.

This happened after we aired several stories in which Jerry exposed a well-known General Motors dealership for pulling Delco radios—which were the standard in the industry—out of their cars and allegedly replacing them with Japanese radios. At the time, Japanese radios were generally considered inferior.

The dealership owner was so outraged, he demanded a meeting with the station's general manager. Our GM came out of sales, so he was supportive of our sales department, where this auto dealer spent big bucks. At the same time, our general manager was equally supportive of the news department.

Regardless, I was terrified when the GM told Jerry and myself that we had to attend this meeting, and he warned me in advance that the auto dealer wanted us fired. This was happening in the first year of my career, and the thought of losing the job I loved was devastating.

"I want them fired," the auto dealer told our GM during the meeting that included the news director, Jerry, and myself.

"Why?" the GM asked.

"Why!?" the dealer snarled. "They made me look bad, that's why."

"So is it true?" our general manager asked the dealer, point-blank. "Are you replacing the radios?"

The guy never answered, because he couldn't deny it; he was caught red-handed.

"If you don't fire them, I'm pulling my ads," the dealership owner threatened.

Our GM turned to me and the news director and asked if we covered all our bases in reporting the story. We confirmed that we had. The general manager then turned back to the dealer and told him to get the fuck out of his office, and that he could shove his money up his ass.

The dealership owner walked out, and pulled his ads, as promised. But we were the number one station, so six months later, the dealer's commercials were back on our airwaves.

This story was inspiring because our news department had so much support from top management. I don't think that would happen anymore these days. Sales is so much in bed with news and advertising at some stations that it still drives news product. But whatever the case, I was proud to be part of that investigation at the time it happened.

In 1986 in St. Louis, Susan Akin was crowned Miss America. I received a tip from a federal source that her family was related to the KKK. It wasn't a distant relation either. Her grandfather was, in fact, a suspect in Mississippi for some murders of three civil rights activists during the 1960s. He'd been charged, but was absolved. The whole thing was a major scandal that had been conveniently swept under the rug. Once we exposed the story, major national publications jumped on the story. As for Susan Akin? Amid much controversy, she kept her crown and title as Miss America.

At WJBK, Vince Wade uncovered a story about how Isaiah Thomas had been allegedly involved in high-stakes dice games and other gambling. This was around the time the Pistons won the NBA championship in 1990. The victory elevated the Pistons to hero status; this made me question whether we should run the story.

But to this day, I'm convinced that we were right to air it.

First, we went to the Pistons and told them what we knew. We asked them if they wanted to comment. I sat with my boss, Steve Antoniotti, across the table from Detroit Pistons President and CEO Tom Wilson and Pistons General Manager Jack McCloskey.

"You wouldn't dare run such a story," they said.

"Oh, yes we would," I said.

And so we did. In the days when Vinnie Johnson was being praised for making the winning shot against Portland, we broke the story. This created serious tension. So the Pistons rolled out their public relations machine and asked stations if they wanted to interview Thomas to refute our "outlandish and erroneous charges."

They didn't roll out their hard-hitting reporters, though. Instead, they turned to their anchor people whom they knew would ask soft ball questions. One such anchor interviewed Thomas in his backyard where he played like the saintly superstar many thought he was. Because of this, we took some major hits. The other stations kissed Piston ass.

Then in 1997, the book *Money Players* by Armen Keteyian came out, alleging that Thomas and others were in deep debt from gambling issues. The book finally gave us some satisfaction that, at least publicly, we knew we were right all along.

I don't think I'll ever forget Antoniotti screaming at me about how badly covering that story hurt the station. But ultimately, we knew it was the right thing. And I would have run this story again—even though during the subsequent months and years, I was out at the Palace and got roughed up, slammed up against the wall, and threatened by people who were still angry.

Sick and tired of seeing young Black men and women shot to death—often by members of their own community *in their community*—I decided to do a story called, "When Brother Kills Brother." I was aware of a persistent and dangerous stereotype that white people should be afraid of being shot by Black people. Amidst this is the sad and heart-breaking phenomenon of Black people killing other Black people—hence, brother killing brother.

I called in reporter John Noel and asked him if he felt the same frustration. He looked at me like I was crazy. He really thought I was crazy when I told him I wanted him to go into the hood and knock on the door of every small, medium, and large undertaker. My hope was that he could find an undertaker—preferably an older man or woman—who would be willing to wear a wireless mic and be interviewed by John while embalming the body of someone under 16.

He went out for days and knocked on doors. He found the story, but no one who would wear the mic. Then one day, an older undertaker said he was willing to do it.

This was a man who was no stranger to embalming. It was a routine part of his work. But to hear his voice shake, shiver, and crack while embalming a young Black man was powerful and emotional. And it was precisely what I wanted to get. The result was an award-winning piece that was so moving that it brought the story home. It didn't change things in the neighborhoods. But it informed and shined a spotlight where it had not shone before.

In September of 1985, *Time* magazine ran a story entitled, "When Brother Kills Brother." I saw this as homage; we shed light on a very grim situation.

With all of that said, WXYZ News Director Phil Nye taught me that one of the most courageous things to do was to not run a story sometimes.

A white racist cop who was a police source of mine told me about an organization within the force called WOLFE. It stood for White Officers Looking For Equality. He said they felt put upon and smothered by Coleman Young, who had rid the force of a lot of the rough and renegade cops like him. So one night, this officer told me a cross burning was going to happen in the backyard at one of the cops' homes.

They wore white robes with wolf heads and burned a cross while yelling racist epithets. The wolf heads weren't actual wolf heads, but they were frighteningly real. This was no Halloween party costume, though. Hell, it wasn't even October. These cops were full of hatred and needed to be rooted out. So after the incident, we came out of our truck, confronted the officers, and tried to get them to talk. They refused. Since the officers wouldn't talk and they still wore their wolf heads, we couldn't run the story because we had no proof who they were.

We also went to meetings with the big bosses at ABC and they were determined that the story would never see the light of day. And it never did.

But I still have the video in my drawer.

COVERAGE MOTIVATED BY "WHAT WOULD GEORGE AND MARTHA THINK?"

I had the good fortune to win many awards and nominations

during my career. The greatest award or reward for me, though, was always airing stories that helped our viewers and that effected change. These two components were critical.

For me, it was always about "George and Martha"—the everyday people who were viewers at home. If a story was bad, I'd say, "That's a fucking piece of shit. I'm sure George is turning to Martha and saying, 'What the fuck is that?'" But when you gave George and Martha a story with a benefit, it meant something.

A good news team knows how to do good journalism while providing infotainment and still making a profit. At the end of the day, I knew my team could do it all.

What I've found anecdotally over the years, however, is that oftentimes, the newsrooms that are winning the awards are usually in last place ratings-wise because they don't focus on the most important thing—the viewer. I knew what the viewers wanted, because I talked with them and, maybe more importantly, they talked with us. They kept coming back, again and again. You either had the feel or you didn't. Phil Nye had always said, "Take it to the people, to the neighborhoods." I carried that theme throughout my career.

AGENT OF CHANGE

After WJBK, I had several offers to stay in broadcasting. But I knew I'd had enough. During my last few years at the station, things had gone sour for me. I never quit because I was making a lot of money and it was hard to bid farewell to that. But I'd drive to work praying that I'd be fired and that they'd offer me a big buyout.

Actually, they offered me a $100,000 buyout, but I turned it down. It wasn't enough. So they just kicked me out with nothing. I hired a lawyer and filed an EEOC (U.S. Equal Employment Opportunity Commission) claim exposing some members of local management at WJBK as racist, sexist, bigoted, and homophobic. The claim was dismissed twice.

We eventually went back and negotiated with corporate attorneys. It would take a year for me to get the money I initially asked for. It wasn't the money so much that was the issue. I just felt it was really important to expose some members of local management for being bigots, racists, sexists, and homophobes—in addition to my own issues.

In the meantime, I started working as a media trainer. And I wrote a book about how to get positive stories and neutralize negative stories. I knew this would take a very long time to build. I also created a public relations crisis management seminar.

While working in crisis management, I met with the Israeli cabinet in Washington D.C. They wanted me to train them on how to talk to the media in both Israel and on a global platform. My late friend Tripp Frohlichstein connected me with them. It was something he did often when he had too much work. I think their willingness to meet with me was also aided by my being Jewish. Most of them appeared to hang on every word I said. They were hungry for resolve. Not surprising, given they hail from a country that is forever seeking resolution.

Over time, I would work with doctors, lawyers, and university educators in this same capacity. And though it may not come as a big surprise, I often found doctors to be the most resistant.

On the agent end, I took in only $27,000 that first year. And I did it from my house. This was the day of cassette tapes—not even CDs. So I typed letters and dropped off my tapes at two o'clock in the morning. I was on the phone a lot. But it was working. I eventually moved to a building on Woodward, where I worked as an agent for almost 18 years. During that time, I also launched a cannabis marketing business. When the landlord discovered I was in this line of work, however, a conflict of interest arose, and I moved to my own building in Royal Oak.

The initial round of talent I represented were mostly folks who were either brand new, or who didn't meet the aesthetic requirements. Yeah, it might sound shallow to say that. Yet it's just the reality of being in front of the camera. There is truth to the saying, "a face for radio."

One person who stood out among that early talent was Craig Nigrelli. When I met Craig, he had aspirations to become an anchor, but felt his agent didn't believe in him. I recognized he was rough around the edges, but believed he could do it. So he fired his agent and I quickly got him a morning anchor job. Of the large pool of talent I now represent, Craig continues to be with me. Today he is an anchor in Wichita.

As I became more established as an agent, I was frequently approached by those not in the broadcasting industry who were looking to change jobs. Irika Sargent was one of those people. She called me a number of years ago and said she was a Wall Street attorney and was interested in becoming an anchor woman. I recognized that she had all the necessary elements to succeed as an anchor, but it would take some time.

"You'll have to be okay with taking a major pay cut," I told her.

Irika agreed. She started in a small market in the south, moved up to Houston, then eventually Miami. Now in Chicago, she's the top female anchor, both in background and credibility. Not everyone has been as great as Irika, though.

I once repped a reporter whom I secured a big-city anchor job paying $100,000 per year. This reporter owed me $7,000 and as months went by, she kept giving excuses about why she wasn't paying. I finally got her on the phone and asked when she was going to make her first payment.

"I'm sorry, Mort," she said. "My grandma has been sick and I've just been overwhelmed with everything. I will pay you next month."

Well, I wasn't about to come down on her and demand payment, given her situation.

But the next month, she gave me the same excuse. This went on for several months until she told me her granny died and she would have to pay for the funeral. I didn't want to challenge it because, what if she really had died?

But six months passed and she still hadn't paid. So I contacted her again. She said she still couldn't pay me. "Granny had her other leg amputated," she said. That clinched it.

"They must have dug up her body to do it," I said to her.

It was amazing. She couldn't even keep her lies straight. So I sued her and eventually prevailed.

I had another client whom I'd have been better off avoiding. He was an average sort from another state, who hired me to find him an anchor job—which, of course, I did. But as time went on, he never paid me. No excuses, no dying grandmother who needed to be exhumed. He just wouldn't pay. Since he owed me a considerable amount, I sued him.

The lawsuit was in Michigan. All of my contracts are written on Michigan law. If I sue someone, they need to come to Michigan. So even though you won the case in Michigan, it was a hollow victory. He defaulted and they ruled against him. His lawyer in his home state most likely told him, forget it. You don't have to pay. My hands were tied. So I had no choice but to let it go.

Then many years later, he called me out of the blue. He claimed he had a dream wherein Jesus told him that he needed to pay me my debt.

"So how much do I owe you?" he asked.

I told him it was $15,000, but that I'd take $10,000 in a cashier's check. He sent it and, amazingly enough, the funds were good. It was nothing short of a miracle.

Or so it seemed.

Two weeks later, my collection attorney got a call from him, saying that he'd paid me the money and was wondering if my attorney would write a letter to his creditors stating that the debt had been settled. He needed this matter cleared up, because he was being blocked from getting a mortgage. Unless his mortgage was being supplied by Jesus, he'd been caught in a lie. But at least I got paid.

As an agent, I shoot straight and tell it like it is. I still represent a good guy and excellent talent by the name of Steve Shaw. He had the makings of a great anchor, but had a drinking problem. So I only agreed to represent him if he agreed to clean up his life. He was motivated, and quit drinking. I got him an interview in Minneapolis—

where he landed the job. When we both saw the ax budget, he jumped from Minneapolis before getting chopped. He now lives in Oklahoma and has stayed clean.

One day, I received a call from a man who was inquiring about becoming an anchorman. I couldn't tell his age, but guessed he was probably in his 30s or 40s.

"Sure, I'd be happy to talk to you," I said.

"Alright," he said. "See, I'm a bank manager in Detroit and I'm ready to do something else."

"Hmmm," I said. "Okay. So then what makes you think you're qualified to be a news anchor?"

"I've been watching guys like Bill Bonds and Mort Crim for years. Honestly, it doesn't seem all that tough."

I agreed to meet with him—which is what I usually do. One, because I like people, and two, because you never know what you might find. He could have been the next Bill Bonds. Or perhaps he was a total crackpot. Either way, we set up a time for him to visit my office.

At the appointed time, he showed up. He appeared to be around 40—handsome with a great voice and a big smile. He seemed promising. I offered him a seat and asked for his demo reel.

"Sure," he said, handing it to me. I popped it into my computer to watch it. Now, I generally have an 18-second rule, whereby I can tell if someone has the right stuff, so to speak. So after that 18 seconds, I popped it out and asked my visitor if he had a thick skin or thin skin.

"I'd say it's thick," he said with confidence.

"Good," I said, looking him straight in the eyes. "That was one of the worst, if not the very worst demo, I have ever seen." I then held the reel in two hands, snapped it, and dropped it in my garbage can. "I suggest you keep your job as a bank manager and I truly wish you well."

It sounds cold, I know. Yet, he took my words surprisingly well.

He stood and thanked me. Then as he walked to the door, he turned and said, "Thanks so much for your time."

That was the end of that. Or at least I thought… until two hours later when I received another call. This time it was a woman and she quickly identified herself as the sister of the man I'd seen earlier that day.

She had some choice words for me that essentially broke down to the fact that I was a son of a bitch who had shattered her brother's dreams. Then she hung up.

The next morning when I came into my office, my assistant at the time, Kristie, had posted a sign on my door that said, MORT MEISNER—SHATTERER OF DREAMS.

It's still prominently displayed to this day.

A female anchor was one of my early clients who's now divorced from a leach of a husband. Back when I met her in Kansas City, her husband—who called me "friend" all the time— asked if we could go out for an expensive dinner. So I took the whole family out; the husband even asked for a to-go order for the next night. The woman bounced around quite a bit and she didn't pay me. So I had to sue her.

Tom Jordan is an Emmy Award-winning radio guy in Detroit and I repped him when he lived in San Diego. One day, I got a call from Debbie Kenyon, who used to manage all the CBS stations. She said she needed a morning anchor. I told her I represented mostly TV people, but I had a guy with "big pipes" in San Diego who might be a good fit. His wife didn't even want to visit Detroit, let alone live there. But we convinced her to give it a shot.

While I was working with Tom, he sheepishly said that he was afraid I'd be mad at him, but he told me that he hadn't had the nerve to tell me that he wasn't Jewish every year when I sent him Hanukkah cards.

Even as my agent business began to thrive, I had difficulty finding good assistants. In fact, I had a string of truly *Murphy Brown* types. My first assistant sometimes hid the tapes behind the couch rather than mail them. This obviously wasn't good for business. Other assistants would be hungover, late, or plagued by personal problems. For a long time, the average lifespan of an assistant with me was about two years.

It didn't deter me. I enjoy the agency business, because I love finding talent—even young talent coming out of college. At the beginning, when they start their careers in small markets with low salaries, my commission is small, but this changes as they ascend the ranks into bigger markets. I represent talent in more than 40 states and get solicited dozens of times per week from people at all levels in the industry.

I love being an agent and plan to do it for a long time.

FAMILY TIES

It's been said that family ties are the ones that bind. And gag.

Well, as far as my dad was concerned, I spent much of my childhood in a chokehold from his anger. And though my relationship with my mother was better, it was hardly sterling. In either case, though, I was beholden to them. Especially as they aged. They were my parents.

My mother was the daughter of Hungarian immigrants who emigrated to New York and then to Detroit in the 1930s. My mother's father was in the laundry business and lost everything in the crash of 1929. He died a month before I was born.

My father's father was a tough, strident, and brutal man who headed the Baker's Union in Detroit. My father's mother was sickly. My father had a brother, Sam, an optometrist who was shell-shocked from the war. He was permitted to attend college, while my father was not. My father's sister, Gertrude, was also college-educated.

Then there was my brother, Tony.

My earliest memories of my brother go back to when I was three or four and he was 12 or 13. He was very doting and loved to play with me. He would get a little rough at times—body slamming me when we wrestled. My mother used to yell at him to stop.

When he went off to college, his absence felt like a hole had opened up in my life. But he wouldn't be gone at college for long. He soon came home because he was "sick." (In retrospect, I think he had a nervous breakdown; sadly, only the first of many incidents—including suicide attempts—he'd experience as he got older.)

Tony did continue with school. He lived back at home with my parents and me while he attended Wayne State University in Detroit. Eventually he got a master's degree, then went on to law school. And he always found time for me.

I don't have many bright memories of my childhood. But I do remember one day with particular fondness. In 1966, right before my bar mitzvah, I was standing on the front porch of my house and glanced down the street. Off in the distance, a guy was riding a bike, and pulling another bike alongside of him. It was a strange scene, to be sure.

As he came around the curb and got closer to the house, he seemed familiar. It was Tony! Given that my parents could not (or would not) get me a bike for my bar mitzvah, he took it upon himself to do so. It was a purple Schwinn Varsity and it was just about the most beautiful thing I'd ever seen.

My brother is the namesake for my grandson.

Shortly after my father died in 1985, my mother was attacked in her home and subsequently had a stroke. The authorities never did find the guys. But the police suspected it was someone who'd been to the house before. The thing about my mom was that she trusted people. She'd always let people—even complete strangers—into her house to give them cookies and brownies. It was heart-breaking to move her out of her house, but she couldn't be there alone any longer. We found a nursing home in Livonia and settled her into a room there.

Three years later, in 1988, I was settling back into Detroit with Leslie. We decided it was time to build a family. It would not come easy. We tried for four years and were having no luck conceiving.

During that time, my mother's condition slowly worsened.

On June 24th of 1992, I was driving back from a Chicago visit when my intuition said I should visit my mother. I walked into her room and she was laying on her left side, staring into space.

"Mom," I said gently. "It's Mort."

She turned over and looked at me. But she didn't say a word. She turned away from me.

The next morning, I was playing softball when I received the call that she was gone. Oddly, I felt the need to return to the field to finish the game.

It was a dark and overcast day. But when I ran out to left field, the sun briefly came out. It still sends goosebumps down my spine when I think about it. When the game was over, I returned to the nursing home. I noted that her wedding ring was gone. Stolen, I presumed. We never saw it again.

A couple of months later in August, early on a Saturday morning, I received a call from my friend and employee at work, Murray Feldman.

"I know it's none of my business that you and Leslie have been trying to have kids and haven't had any success," he said, then paused. "Have you considered adoption?"

We hadn't.

He said that his sister-in-law, Judy, had adopted a child out of Kansas and they knew of someone else whose 15-year-old daughter was pregnant and would be putting the baby up for adoption.

Though we hadn't considered adoption before, it made sense. After all, we wanted a baby. And the opportunity was presenting itself. We pondered it for a couple of days, then called Murray to get more information.

Five days after that, we were on our way to Philadelphia to meet the birth mother, Nicole, her mother, Sue, and the birth father. Then on October 12th, 1992, we got the call that Nicole was going into labor. Leslie and I jumped on a plane to Kansas City, Missouri, then raced to the hospital in Lawrence, Kansas. The reason Nicole was having the child in Kansas was that she had been harassed by the birth father, who had threatened her with bodily harm. Nicole and her mother had moved to Kansas to live with an uncle in order to keep her out of harm's way until the baby was born.

When the baby was born, we chose to name her Nicole because we loved the name and wished to honor her birth mother. We went immediately to court and they granted us temporary custody. We flew home the next day with our beautiful, two-day-old daughter. We thought everything was complete at that point. We had only to return 30 days later to finalize the adoption in court.

When we returned to Missouri for what we thought would be a simple termination of rights hearing, we were informed that the birth father had changed his mind. This started a three-state, two-year, $150,000 legal battle. While no longer able to practice law, my ever-vigilant brother helped in any way he could, offering his legal expertise. He even sold his blood and plasma to help pay our legal fees. The case went all the way to the Supreme Court in Kansas and changed child's rights laws in Michigan. But at times, I thought the mountain was going to collapse.

We even had contingencies to hide our Nicole, if need be, in Canada. Fortunately, none of that happened and we eventually prevailed. I can say with certainty that it was the best money I ever spent—having the honor of raising our wonderful daughter.

As is often the case, just two weeks after we brought Nicole home, Leslie learned she was finally pregnant. And nine months later, Nicole's brother Mark was born.

For as wonderful as my brother was, I would be lying if I said he was the one stable element in my family. I was certainly indebted to him for protecting me as a child and always helping me when he could. In fact, he enjoyed many years of professional and financial success.

The truth is, though, it was never easy with Tony. From day to day, you never knew which Tony you'd find. Sometimes he was Casanova. Other times you'd encounter Filthy McNasty. It was difficult to separate the lies from truth with my brother.

It turns out that Tony had an undiagnosed illness. It took many years to recognize that he suffered from bipolar disorder. This would eventually lead to an addiction—which I understood all too well. Guilt, shame, and a way to kill the pain were what had driven my drugging 15 years earlier.

Perhaps a part of his mental condition, Tony was famous for being a hypochondriac and frequently shopped doctors. When he started having some back pain, he went to six or seven surgeons to inquire about back surgery. Not one of them felt he was a candidate. He finally found a young surgeon who agreed to do surgery he didn't need. With the surgery and the wounds came a lot of narcotics. It didn't take long before he was addicted to opioids.

Everyone who loved Tony wanted him to stop and tried to get him help. Nothing was working, though. After many failed attempts to help him, his wife had to kick him to the curb.

During the last six months of his life, he was so severely addicted and such a compulsive liar, I had to cut him off, too. The last time I saw my brother alive was in February of 2001, when he got out of his car at Starr Bakery. It tore my heart out not to run to my big brother and give him a hug. For my own self-preservation, I knew I couldn't. Instead, I drove away.

When his son, Andy, called me two months later to tell me Tony had died, I was not surprised. We'll never know if he died from a heart attack from his addiction or from suicide. When you get right down to it, it was suicide either way.

At my brother's funeral, I turned the eulogy into a speech about mental illness. I was angry and hurt and wanted to take the stigma off that exists around mental illness.

Tony died on April 1st—April Fool's Day. Strangely enough, years earlier I had also lost my dear friend Nelson to cancer on that date, as well as another friend in 2019. I'm not sure what that means, if anything.

In terms of time with my family, my being let go from WJBK in 1997 had a silver lining. I was able to spend more time with Mark and Nicole.

As the kids continued to grow, I loved being a father. I now had time to coach Mark's baseball team, which only further strengthened the bond I already had with my son. I threw him batting practice 46 weeks per year. I watched him blossom into a great player and he eventually realized his dream of playing Division One Baseball. He's now an agent for the Major League.

Meanwhile, Nicole was proving to be a gifted runner. Although I was not able to coach her in her sport, I traveled to watch her run at meets throughout the country and even the world. She was one of the best sprinters ever at University of Detroit Mercy and broke national and international records when she competed.

Sadly, Jason grew up mostly away from me and I didn't get to spend more than one weekend per month with him. Jason's mother and I divorced when he was between one and two years old. It was tough. In fact, it was one of the biggest heartbreaks of my life. I didn't get to spend enough time with him during his formative years. Even as he got older, I still only saw him every other month. It was never enough.

Jason is now an incredibly successful business man running restaurants in Maryland. If I could do it again, I'd have found a way to be there more for him.

So it was no big surprise that when my kids started moving into their own adult lives, I felt deeply sad. But it forced me to figure out how to find value in my own life. Much of this began with looking back into my childhood and the incidents that shaped me.

For as much damage as he caused, my dad had a remarkable sense of humor. Not many people know he was also a great cartoonist. Like many of us though, he just couldn't step out of his own way.

It's clear now that TV news had been an emotional outlet for me. It was a place to let out some steam. Some days, it was a lot of steam.

Of course, the cocaine use for seven or eight years was a response to that. But I also wanted to hide my shame, mask my pain, and cover my guilt. No amount of cocaine could do that. I'd snort lines while sitting on the toilet, make midnight runs to pick up cocaine, or even be down on my knees picking cocaine out of the shag carpeting (also known as crumbing).

If I had the option to do it again, I'd change things. It happened, however, and I can't go back. I know I don't need to punish myself any longer, even though some people in my life still speak to me about it in a punishing sort of way.

I try not to let it bother me or get me down, but I'd be lying if I said it didn't.

These days, I recognize how much of my life has been—and continues to be—fear-based. Even now, I worry about what tomorrow will bring. The real bad stuff is in the rearview mirror, though. Yeah, I still have a streak of obsessive-compulsiveness—where I know something is not a good idea, but I do it anyway. But I'm human. That's why I continue to seek and receive help. I am much better and more focused. I recognize the value of taking it one day at a time.

I still work hard, but don't play as hard as I'd like to. I love, but don't feel as loved as I'd like to be. I don't feel I receive the respect I've earned. And though I give for the sheer joy of giving, I recognize that I always give too much.

While I don't expect anything back, I'd be lying if I said it wouldn't be nice.

AND BRUCE SPRINGSTEEN IS *STILL* MY HERO

Circling back to Bruce Springsteen, the *Ghost of Tom Joad Tour* in 1997 was phenomenal. In the course of three days, I saw three different shows that will forever stay in my mind.

It began on a Monday night when I went to see Springsteen in Cleveland. I was meeting my best friend Jim there—who was coming up from Texas for the show. By this time, I'd already seen numerous shows with Jim, who is almost as ravenous a Springsteen fan as I am. In fact, we'd seen our first show on tour in Chicago, and after that, we'd hook up in different cities to see him.

Springsteen was playing Monday and Tuesday night in Cleveland and I had tickets for both shows. Jim was only planning to be there on Monday night, because he'd brought his son Jimmy, and they had to get back to Texas the following day. The Monday night show ended up being all acoustic. Even so, it was a great show. There's really no such thing as a bad Springsteen show.

After Jim and his son departed on Tuesday, I was left to my own devices. So I went to the mall and wandered around for a bit. I found a spot in the food court and settled in to read *The Grapes of Wrath*—the 1939 John Steinbeck novel whose character Tom Joad inspired the name of the Grammy Award-winning album. Then, who do I see but Bruce walking around the food court. It was about 11 a.m. He saw me and nodded, then walked up to me.

By this time, I'd come to know most of the band members. Bruce, however, only knew me by sight and rarely remembered I'd promoted him unless I reminded him. So I was surprised, and admittedly moved, when he asked where Nelson was. I was amazed that he remembered my dear friend who had died two years earlier in 1995.

I shared with him the news of his passing and told him that in Nelson's eulogy, I'd read the lyrics to *No Retreat, No Surrender,* and *Bobbie Jean.* Tears came down his face.

"How about a Coke?" he offered.

Was I gonna turn down having a Coke with the Boss? So we sat down and talked and I told him what a great show it had been. He asked if I had tickets for that night and I told him that I did indeed have one ticket. He looked at me and shook his head.

"I want you in the first row," he said. "Go to my road manager's room and ask for two tickets."

Sure enough, when I went to George Travis' room, there were two tickets for me—front row and center.

Bruce came out and the first song was *The Ghost of Tom Joad.* He spent hours doing most, if not all, of the album, left the stage, did a few encores, then said, "I'll be right back." He came back out with a chair and put it in front of me. Then he started tuning his guitar.

He looked up and said, "I'm gonna do a song right now I haven't done on this tour and I'm dedicating it to Mort and his friend Nelson who's up there," and he pointed to the sky. He sang *No Retreat, No Surrender.* It sent chills up and down my spine. At the end of the show, he nodded to me and motioned for me to come backstage.

When I got to the stage door, the manager asked what I wanted.

"Bruce invited me backstage," I said. He let me through and Bruce approached me. He put his arm around me and said, "Thanks for letting me know about that. It meant a lot to me."

After I left Bruce, I went out into the cold December and called

Nelson's wife, Glenda. I told her about what had happened and his tribute to Nelson.

We both cried.

That Wednesday night, Bruce was scheduled to play in St. Louis. Jim and I had tickets for that show, too. I was supposed to fly there, but the weather had grown increasingly inclement during the night on Tuesday and into Wednesday morning.

Given that I'd been in a helicopter crash in 1979, I was already apprehensive about flying. I wasn't ready to step on a plane in the midst of a mixed bag of wintry weather. I was, however, willing to get into a car and drive through it. And since it was early enough on Wednesday morning, I made the arrangements to get a car and started my journey to the town which had once been my home.

I hit every kind of weather on the way there, but I made it. Since this was before the days when everyone had cell phones, I had to stop many times along the way to call Jim and let him know where I was.

Once I finally arrived at the venue, exhausted but equally excited, I discovered the tickets were again in the front row.

Now, *The Ghost of Tom Joad Tour* was always very somber. Despite the audience cheering and calling out what they wanted to hear, Bruce would typically ask people to be quiet. That night, he was a bit more playful. When he saw me in the front row, he said aloud, "Man, don't you have a fucking job!?"

Nobody else in the audience knew what he was talking about. It was our own inside joke. He proceeded to do the show, with another tribute to Nelson at the end. I was truly taken.

It was an amazing 48 hours and one of the most moving experiences of my life. Because that's the kind guy Bruce was, is, and always will be.

No life is perfect. Like everyone walking this planet, I've had my share of defeats and losses. Still, I've also had a life full of excitement and with many loves. I can say with certainty that learning to love Bruce helped me learn to love many other musicians. If I'm being honest, it may have even taught me to love myself a little.

And that's saying a lot.

THE BEST OF THE BEST

How can you write a book about the world of TV news without having a Best Of section? So without further ado, the award goes to...

BEST MALE ANCHOR

Bill Bonds, who I worked with at both WXYZ and WJBK in Detroit, was a Detroit original, if not an American original. While not a success in Los Angeles or New York, Billy killed it in the Motor City. He had a way of taking the worst day and making it better with the great read of a newscast closer. With his amazing memory, great writing skills, and endless talent, Billy owned the Detroit airwaves.

BEST MALE ANCHOR RUNNER-UP

Huel Perkins, who worked with me at KSDK in St. Louis and WJBK in Detroit. The late critic Bob Talbert once said that Perkins wouldn't last 18 months in Detroit, and he was right. Huel's going on 30 years now. Talented, thoughtful, and socially conscious, Huel asks tough questions and leads by example.

BEST FEMALE ANCHOR

Diana Lewis left KABC in Los Angeles for greener pastures at WXYZ in Detroit during the summer of 1977. Always a team player, Diana was well-read and brought a sense of fairness and balance to the news.

She could get anyone to do an interview because everyone trusted her. And with good reason.

BEST FEMALE ANCHOR RUNNER-UP

Karen Foss of KSDK in St. Louis was originally perceived as something of an ice queen. But as we worked with her, the iciness melted and she blossomed into an amazing anchor and a great reader. She became a star in her own right—sporting a hairstyle that became so popular in St. Louis, it was simply known as the Foss.

BEST MALE REPORTER

Jay Levine of WLS in Chicago had a ferocity not only to win and beat the competition senseless, but to cover every major story without ever making it about him. Jay loved to be in the field and to dig. He was demanding and even intimidating. But he owned his stories 100 percent. If I had to stake my career on one reporter bringing it home, that reporter would be Jay Levine.

BEST MALE REPORTER - RUNNER-UP

Scott Lewis of WJBK in Detroit was one of those rare talents who came out of radio to become a major success on television. Whether doing investigative work or general stories on the street, Scott was aggressive, but also painstakingly careful.

BEST FEMALE REPORTER

Kathryn Kiefer of WXYZ could investigate and break loose the rapes and murders of women in Detroit one day, then do a stellar job covering a story on an overturned truck of pigs the next. Kathryn had an attitude and an edge. Successful in Chicago, Boston, San Francisco, Denver, and St. Louis, she could write a story and deliver it with a sense of urgency greater than most, and better than all I worked with before and after.

BEST FEMALE REPORTER - RUNNER-UP

Terry Anzur of WBBM worked with me in an age where female reporters who pushed back would automatically be disliked by management. As such, she was often berated. But she kept coming back and doing a great job.

BEST CRIME REPORTER

John "Bulldog" Drummond was at WBBM in Chicago full time from 1969 to 1997, but continued to break stories, and chase the mafia, low-level gangsters, and even Nazi War Criminals until he retired in 2014. Whether chasing Joey "the clown" Lombardo with his sidekick, James "Legs" D'Antonio, Anthony "Big Tuna" Accardo or Joseph "Doves" Aiuppa, John was a remarkable reporter and gumshoe. He was colorful, smart, and simply the best.

BEST CRIME REPORTER - RUNNER-UP

Ven Marshall of WXYZ Detroit often sported a handlebar mustache and had an Edward R. Murrow-like delivery. He covered crime and labor with unparalleled wile. When asked how he was doing, his standard response was, "Everything is so fucking beautiful, even I can't believe it." He was highly respected, honored, and loved by the industry.

BEST SPORTSCASTER

Dave Diles is the best sportscaster I've had the pleasure of working with and knowing. Dave did sports on local TV and radio, but he also worked for ABC Sports at the highest level. Unlike many sportscasters today, Dave was not afraid to confront management, athletes, and owners to get the best story. When Dave joined WXYZ, it meant to me that we had the Dean of all sportscasters in the United States.

BEST SPORTSCASTER - RUNNER-UP

Johnny Morris of WBBM in Chicago was hard-working with a great sense of humor, along with an awesome laugh—especially when Gene Siskel was holding up pornographic photographs in the middle of his sportscast, which Siskel would often do.

BEST METEOROLOGIST

Jerry Hodak, who started at WJBK, went to WXYZ, then returned to WJBK, was Mr. Reliable when it came to school bell weather. Smooth, polished, and professional, this Chief Meteorologist found no glee in scaring the hell out of viewers. He was also a high-quality health and science reporter.

BEST METEOROLOGIST - RUNNER-UP

John Coughlin of WBBM was also smooth and polished, but rarely talked to folks in the newsroom outside of weather. Nevertheless, he was beloved.

BEST BUSINESS AND FINANCE ANCHOR/REPORTER

Murray Feldman, who was my Business Reporter at WJBK in Detroit, is far and away the best Business and Finance Anchor/Reporter I ever worked with. Murray had a way of taking complicated stories and simplifying them. He could explain them so well that every "George and Martha" at home would understand them. Murray also had a Rolodex like you wouldn't believe, containing presidents of auto companies, banks, and many other large and small corporations. Murray was, and always has been, the epitome of a team player. When it came to business reporting, Murray had no rivals.

BEST FEATURE REPORTER

John Pertzborn from KSDK in St. Louis could interview a tree and make it interesting. He was that funny and that good. He even did an interesting story on an underwater monopoly tournament. That's right, underwater monopoly. John eventually left the station and became an anchor in St. Louis at KTVI, where he does a great job. John was so witty and funny. Well-liked with no peer, not anywhere, not ever.

BEST FEATURE REPORTER - RUNNER-UP

Erik Smith of WXYZ could cover any story in any category. From pigeon races to ice carving contests, Eric would inject himself and have everyone rolling in the newsroom and at home. He was a brilliant hard news reporter as well. Eric knew how to find the interview nobody else considered, then let the people tell the story.

BEST MULTI-PLATFORM INVESTIGATOR

Vince Wade had better federal connections than anyone else with whom I ever worked. Vince and I worked together at WXYZ and I thought so highly of him I brought him to WJBK to help turn around our newsroom. He was hardboiled and sometimes arrogant and combative. But I loved him. Wade covered the big stories—Hoffa, Coleman Young, you name it. Not liked by all, he was undeniably a top gun reporter.

BEST BOSS/NEWS DIRECTOR/GENERAL MANAGER

Steve Antoniotti who I worked with at WXYZ in Detroit, KSDK in St. Louis, and WJBK in Detroit, gave me a chance after being out of the business for a year. Although sometimes explosive, Steve was always kind and compassionate. A great man, a smart man, and a friend for life. Steve would often describe himself as "tough but fair." He was right.

BEST BOSS/NEWS DIRECTOR - RUNNER-UP

Bill Applegate was a ferocious leader and warrior. He knew only one way and that was to win. Bill specialized in turning stations around with his battle cry, "This is war!" And it usually was. Bill was smart, crafty, and a winner. But I learned from him what not to do, just as much as what to do.

BEST MALE EXECUTIVE PRODUCER

Larry Perret was brilliant and fastidious, always wanting "more news." He knew how to build a newscast, and whatever Larry touched generally turned to gold. To this day, his scorecard shows far more wins than losses. Also, a news director in Los Angeles and Atlanta, Larry was dapper, smart, and so talented.

BEST FEMALE EXECUTIVE PRODUCER

Ava Ehrlich has to be the smartest person I have ever met. She's also one of the nicest and classiest. Ava knew the news, as well as how to manage people. She could analyze, deploy, and commit resources to a story as well as or better than anyone I have ever known.

BEST CONSULTANT

Joe Rovitto is a shining star in a business where everyone who isn't in the newsroom seems to be a consultant. Always prepared, Joe was a picture of knowledge, information, and class. He's the proverbial real deal and a top-notch consultant with only my best interests at heart.

BEST MULTI-PLATFORM MANAGER

Tom Bell at WJBK was an incredibly organized manager with a brilliant analytical mind. He would keep me apprised on what was going on in the newsroom as we quietly did the countdown for my return to Detroit. With a brilliant analytical mind, and a nose for news, he went to war with me each and every morning as we rallied to bring WJBK back to life.

BEST POLITICAL REPORTER

Mike Flannery of WBBM in Chicago was the top political reporter with whom I had the pleasure of working. Hailing from a background in newspaper, if there was a major story at city hall or at the state capitol in Springfield, Mike had it, broke it, and did a great job telling it.

BEST POLITICAL REPORTER - RUNNER-UP

Hugh Hill at WLS was known as Agent Orange, due to the terrible hair dye jobs he frequently had done that made the sides of his head orange. Hugh knew everyone and they all knew him. With an extensive list of contacts, he could find out anything and report on it.

BEST ASSISTANT

Tom Sides was a real-life Kentucky Colonel. Tom brought with him a wealth of knowledge and history of the TV news industry and was one of a small handful of people who always felt confident in telling me what I needed, as opposed to what he thought that I wanted to hear. A great sidekick and honorable TV newsman, he was pivotal in the revival of WJBK.

Mort has been recognizing, developing and honing talent in the news industry for more than 30 years. With direct experience as a major market news director, assistant news director, investigative producer, managing editor, and assignment editor, Mort has knowledge of all aspects of the broadcast news world.

In an industry driven by competition, he is known as an honest critic and an honest businessman. Always direct and fair in his critiques, Mort tells clients what they need to hear. This is often not the case, as many agents will say almost anything in order to get a contract signed. Working with Mort is working with a powerhouse of a personality. Mort has a big presence, a big voice, and a big heart. He is respected for his ethical treatment of his colleagues and clients.

Recognized as an industry expert, Mort is frequently quoted with regard to the news media and is cited in college textbooks on the subject. Many of today's decision makers, news directors and general managers, worked with or for Mort during the span of his career. Relationships drive this business and since Mort has the advantage of knowing so many key players personally, he can reach them directly and gets honest feedback on talent.

Working with talent is in his blood. Right out of high school, with endless energy and an eye for talent, Mort began working in the rock music industry, honing his skills as a promoter. Some of the biggest names pay tribute to Mort as seminal in their successes. Names like KISS, Aerosmith, Bruce Springsteen and Elton John, owe some of their early bookings to his natural networking and development skills. Rock 'n' Roll by night and school by day, Mort studied journalism and communications at the University of Detroit, and in the late 70's, shifted his career path to the highly competitive broadcast news industry. Today, Mort's high energy and vision help some of the nation's most gifted on-air talent develop and further their careers.

Mort has always been a hands-on working journalist. In the 80's and 90's, he orchestrated numerous undercover and investigative stories. In the early 80's at WBBM (CBS) in Chicago, he worked closely with legendary crime reporter John "Bull Dog" Drummond, investigating the infamous Chicago Mafia. In 1985, Mort made national news while in St. Louis during the TWA Flight 847 Hostage Crisis. He scored exclusive live interviews from Lebanon with Amal militia leaders and was the first to orchestrate interviews with some of the hostages after their release, as he flew to Boston with now NBC correspondent Ann Thompson. It is a tribute to Mort that both the hostages and their families trusted him.

In 1988, working out of Detroit's CBS station, Mort traveled to Rome to cover the installation of Bishop Szoka as Cardinal. Always one step ahead, Mort landed an exclusive interview with Pope John Paul II. Mort is a great investigator and information seeker. All of which translates to his expertise as a TV news agent – he seeks out, recognizes, and helps talent reach their full potential.

During his career, Mort earned numerous Emmy awards. Among his awards, Mort won the Emmy for Outstanding News Cast in 1986 as Assignment Manager at KSDK in St. Louis. And in Detroit, in 1995 as News Director at WJBK, Mort won an Emmy for "Breaking Story – Kerrigan Attack;" he uncovered the details of Olympic Skaters Nancy Kerrigan's and Tanya Harding's personal and public conflict during the 1994 Olympics. Mort remained as News Director at WJBK until 1997, taking the station from a CBS Affiliate to a FOX O&O (Owned and Operated). Mort and his management team were responsible for putting together one of the first multiple-hour morning newscasts in the country.

In his personal life, Mort is a committed family man with a lifelong passion for baseball–he has played or coached baseball most of his adult life. So, it is no surprise that when his own children began to play, he became their coach as well. Volunteering his time as a baseball coach, he has helped develop the skills and talents of many young players in his community, many of whom have become division one athletes, including his own 19-year-old daughter in track and his and 18-year-old son in baseball. In the sports arena, as in the news business, Mort's keen eye for talent as well as his grooming and coaching skills have helped him create years of award-winning championship teams.

Contact Mort Meisner

Office: 248-545-2222
Email: Mort@MortMeisner.com
Website: MortMeisner.com

Stephanie Ruopp is a graduate of the University of Michigan and a writer who can happily say that she has dipped her toes, and sometimes her entire foot, into blogging, fiction, creative non-fiction, copywriting, screenwriting, and hieroglyphics projects. (The hieroglyphics part is not true, thus proving that she does, in fact, write fiction.) Writing has been the one consistent thread in her ever wavering life. She might even say that it's the thread that's held it all together, though that may well be fiction too. Whatever the case, she's available for writing projects. You can reach her at stephruopp@wordstringer.org.

CPSIA information can be obtained
at www.ICGtesting.com
Printed in the USA
LVHW041720231020
669518LV00003B/195

9 781945 875786